What Christians Believe

What Christians Believe

The Foundation Series
Volume One

by

Kenneth N. Myers

Majeux Press
SHERMAN, TEXAS

What Christians Believe
The Foundation Series, Volume One

© Copyright 2009 by Kenneth N. Myers

Unless otherwise indicated, Scripture is taken from the
HOLY BIBLE, NEW INTERNATIONAL VERSION.
Copyright 1973, 1978, 1984 International Bible Society
Used by permission of Zondervan Bible Publishers.

Myers, Kenneth Neal, 1959-
What Christians Believe/Kenneth N. Myers

ISBN 1-4392-3107-9
LCCN 2009901965

1. Christian Creeds   2. Theology

238

Cover design: Neal Mayeux
Photograph: *El Mesquita, Cordoba Spain* by Neal Mayeux

Published by Mayeux Press
P.O. Box 3497, Sherman, TX 75091

To
My Father, Larry Myers
*who supported me even when he did not understand me
and supports me still now that he does.*

In Loving Memory of
My Father-in-Law, Jerry McSorley
*who once told me I knew nothing about Church history -
and was right.*

Acknowledgements

Thank you to my friends in the Christ Church Cathedral Adult Class which has served as a kind of laboratory for this book and who have enriched it by their questions and insights. A special thank you to Lisa Powell who took very good notes.

Thank you to Scott Rudy and Ken Myers II for proofreading and suggestions.

Thank you to my wife Shirley who is always supportive and who doesn't mind sitting around waiting for me to finish writing so we can go to a late dinner.

Thank you to Don, Tom, Agustin & Lupita at *Hotel Luz en Yucatan* who provided a peaceful haven for writing.

Table of Contents

Preface to the Series

Too many Christians don't know what it really means to be Christian. Some think that "being good" is what it is all about. Some think that holding a general idea about Jesus - that he died for our sins and rose again from the dead - encompasses all that is needed. Too many, in the modern culture, choose to define for themselves the core definitions of the faith: "well, *for me* being a Christian means..." Others say, "Oh, it's all such a bother. I'll just let the clergy worry about that, and I'll go to church and worship God and live my life."

I would suggest (mimicking here the ancient teachings of the Church) that there are four basic considerations Christians need in order to be fully rounded and secure in their faith.

Belief

What you believe matters. As others
have pointed out before me, if you believe five
and five makes ten, and you make a five dollar
purchase and give the cashier a ten dollar bill,
you will not be satisfied with two dollars in
change. Belief matters in the real world. It
defines us, and it defines our relationships
with others - including our relationship with
God. Obviously, belief is not just a religious or
spiritual matter. Belief affects every aspect of
life. If you believe too much sun can cause
skin cancer, you will stay away from too much
sun. If you believe all Cretans are liars, you
won't trust what a Cretan says to you. In the
same way, what you believe about God, Jesus,
the Church, salvation, and the afterlife has an
impact on your every day living, and on your
expectations of the future.

Actions

Actions speak louder that words.
Everyone has heard this axiom. The Christian
faith is not simply a set of theological
statements, it also entails how we *act* in our
lives. Certainly this flows from our beliefs -
real beliefs are played out in what we *do*. Too
often people who consider themselves

Christian do none of the things that follow from true belief.

Saint James wrote, "Show me your faith without deeds, and I will show you my faith by what I *do*...You see that a person is justified by what he *does* and not by faith alone" (James 2.18,24). Just because you say something doesn't necessarily make it so. Actions matter.

Spirituality

Some people hear the word "spirituality" and think of some kind of mystical spookiness, some kind of otherworldiness that causes super-holy others to walk around as if on a cloud. But *everyone* possesses some form of spirituality. By spirituality, I mean how we relate to God in a genuine personal relationship, and how it impacts our relationship with ourselves and with others. The chief means of cultivating a Christian spirituality is through prayer, and yet many believers either do not pray at all, or pray very haltingly, not really knowing *how* to pray.

When we read about godly men and women of the past, we realize they were all people of prayer, including Jesus who, though

he was God come in the flesh, made it his
habit to spend quality time in prayer, and to
teach others how to do the same.

Worship

Finally, Christians who are well-
rounded in their faith are people who worship
God, and they worship God together with
other believers. Far from being a coincidental
aspect of true faith, worshipping God with the
Church is core to what it means to be
Christian. The writer of Hebrews admonished
his readers, "Let us not give up meeting
together, as some are in the habit of doing, but
let us encourage one another - and all the more
as you see the Day approaching" (Hebrews
10.25). Just as in the case of prayer, many
Christians have no idea *how* to worship.
Worship may be seen by some as simply
singing a few songs and listening to a sermon.
Others insist they don't need to gather with
God's people and worship because they can
worship God alone out in nature. Still others
consider themselves too holy to stoop to
gathering with lesser beings and simply stay at
home and "do their own thing", while others
do nothing at all. None of these folk realize
that the Bible has much to say about the
"what" and the "how" of worship.

A Fourfold Plan

I propose four volumes outlining the Christian faith in popular, easy to understand fashion.

Volume One deals with what Christians believe, and focuses on the ancient Creeds of the Church which capsulize true belief.

Volume Two deals with how Christians behave, and focuses on the ethics given by God to Moses in the Ten Commandments.

Volume Three deals with how Christians pray, and focuses on the model Jesus gave his disciples in response to their request that he teach them to pray - the Lord's Prayer or the Our Father.

Volume Four deals with how Christians worship, and focuses on the two aspects of biblical worship: Word and Sacraments.

It should be said that these books are written first and primarily from a Christian perspective which holds the Bible to be the authoritative Word of God and believes that God has moved in his Church and directed it throughout history. It is also written from an Anglican perspective, a viewpoint that sees itself as "Catholic" (that is, rooted in the ancient, undivided faith) and "Protestant" (that is, calling for a continual reformation of the people of God, having the Holy Scriptures as an unerring guide to all matters of belief, action, spirituality and worship). The Anglican faith in one sense finds its roots all the way back with the Apostles, and in another sense finds its roots in the ancient Celtic/British/English church - the church of St. Patrick, St. Columba, St. Hilda, and more recently, influential Christians like C.S. Lewis, J. I. Packer, and a host of others.

If the words of these books have a decidedly Anglican focus, the things to which they speak are much more broad in scope and possess a truth that can be shared by all Christians. My prayer is that these volumes will be used as instruments to enrich all Christians who study them, whatever their denomination or tradition.

Finally, anyone addressing the topics before us - from what Christians believe to how Christians worship - finds himself confronted with an inexhaustible amount of data. Literally millions of sermons on these subjects have been preached over the course of the last 2000 years. Thousands of books have been written about them. The goal of this series is not to be exhaustive, nor even to say everything that is important about the subjects at hand, but to provide a popular level of understanding, thoroughly rooted in Scripture . These books are intentionally designed to be used in personal reading, Sunday School classes, and small group studies. You will notice that the chapters are chock-full of Scriptures. Please do not give in to the temptation to skip over the Scripture texts, thinking you already know what they say. Let them speak to you in a new and fresh way. While I recognize that I can't say everything worthy of being said, I do truly hope that what is written here will stir up minds and hearts and cause people to dig deeper into other resources. I have appended a suggested reading list at the end. What we have before us when we deal with these noble subjects is treasure. It is worth digging for.

Introduction

So, Jolly Old Saint Nick walked up to this guy, his cheeks rosy red - but this time with anger, and smacked him right in the nose! All the onlookers were shocked as the fellow fell to the ground and a nearby policeman arrested Santa and carted him off to jail to cool his pipes overnight.

What have we here? Some twisted Tim Burton retelling of Christmas? A surreal painting by Salvador Dali? Maybe an incomprehensible Bob Dylan song? No, what we have here is the real deal. True History.

The year was 325 and the place was the city of Nicea, in what is now Turkey. More about the scuffle in a minute, but first the backstory.

The Backstory

For three hundred years Christianity had survived and actually thrived, contrary to most expectations, in spite of being hated on all sides. The Jews hated Christianity because in their minds it had kidnapped their religion, which was based on exclusive membership and following the rules, and had turned it into a religion that did away with the rules and flung open the doors to any and all who really wanted to enter. Not only Jews, but Greeks and Romans and Barbarians were turning to the God of Israel and his failure of a Messiah, one Jesus Christ of Nazareth, who had not only failed to be a mighty military deliverer, but had actually died as a common criminal, suffocating to death while nailed to a wooden cross outside Jerusalem, not far from the town dump.

The Roman government also hated Christianity, but for its own, different, reasons. It seems that these followers of Jesus were saying that Caesar wasn't all he was cracked up to be, that he was a mere impostor, and that their Jesus was the true King. All throughout the Roman Empire, from Jerusalem to London, from Greece to Spain, hundreds, then thousands, then hundreds of thousands of people were embracing this upstart religion, and by their lack of allegiance to the Emperor, were threatening the very stability of the Empire itself. And as if that were not enough, many, if not most, of the Christians were from the slave class, and surely this threatened the very structures of civilization. Something had to be done.

The something that was done, it turns out, was persecution. In some times and some places the persecution was relatively mild, with the Christians losing their jobs or maybe being run out of town. In other times and other places it was more severe, with the Christians being tied to poles, soaked in oil, and used as torches to light the chariot races of the Caesar (the original Roman Candles), or sewn up in animal skins and thrown into an arena full of hungry lions, in front of bleachers full of shouting crowds who had paid good money to watch the spectacle, or sent off to the salt mines with harsh working conditions and little food where they were guaranteed an early death from exposure to the elements and starvation.

Then came Constantine. Constantine was a pagan emperor, just like all the Roman Emperors before him, with one difference. He had a praying mom. A *Christian* praying mom. A *British* Christian praying mom. Her name was Helen (later known as *Saint* Helena), and she came from a royal family in Britain which had converted to Christianity as the result of early Christian missionaries. Her father was the noted King Coel of later nursery rhyme fame: "Old King Cole was a merry old soul, and a merry old soul was he..."

In the year 312, the night before a decisive battle at Milvian Bridge, the pagan Emperor Constantine saw a vision of a cross in the sky surrounded by the words, "In Hoc Signo Vinces" - "In This Sign Conquer". Taking it as an omen Constantine ordered his soldiers to paint crosses on their shields and then went off to a merry day of bloodshed in which he defeated his enemy and established himself as the Emperor of the West. Less than a year later he issued an edict (The Edict of Milan) in which Christianity became, for the first time in history, a legal religion.

I'm sure you can imagine the delight of Christians around the world. Put yourself into their shoes. No more hiding, no more worshiping in underground cemeteries, no more being chased out of town, losing jobs or being burned at the stake. Now they could freely worship God in Christ. Now they could build churches. Now they could evangelize without fear.

And so, Christianity continued to grow. But all was not well in Christian-Town for you see, Christianity wasn't a homogeneous group. There were all sorts of things being passed off as "Christian". There were Jewish/Christian sects insisting that one had to follow the Old Testament Law in order to be Christian. There were Gnostic/Christian sects claiming that Jehovah wasn't really God but was an evil impostor, and that Jesus was the Son of the *real* God. There were groups which, under the name of Christianity, said true salvation was found by escaping the bonds of this physical body. And there was a particularly significant group who called themselves Christian, had infiltrated the Church, and were saying that Jesus was *not* God come in the flesh, contrary to the Apostles and the Gospel writers.

No sooner had Constantine made Christianity legal than Christianity itself threatened to fall apart by virtue of ill-definition, and if Christianity fell apart, so would the empire. So in 325 the Emperor called for a meeting of all the Christian bishops where the issues could be hammered out and unity could be achieved. The place was set as Nicea, a lake city not far from Constantine's capital which he modestly named after himself, Constantinople. Over three hundred bishops, along with assistant priests and deacons, traveled from all over the empire for this august occasion. It was presided over by Bishop Hosius of Cordoba, Spain, and the two primary combatants were both from Alexandria, Egypt: a priest named Arius, who claimed that Jesus was not God come in the flesh, and a deacon named Athanasius, who said, "Oh yes, He is!".

Imagine it! Only twelve years earlier Christianity was an outlaw religion. Now the Christian leaders were being invited by the Emperor himself to gather, at his expense, to decide on matters of the faith. The men who walked through the doors of the council room were men who had endured great suffering. Some came on crutches, their legs having been broken in past persecutions. Some came with empty eye sockets, an eye having been gouged out. Some came with missing hands or limbs, or bearing the scars of whips. For a month they met in Nicea to come to terms with what it really meant to be a Christian.

Back to Saint Nick

One of the attendees was the bishop of Myra in Asia Minor (also modern day Turkey) and he was a fierce defender of the true faith. His name was Nicholas of Myra - Saint

Nicholas - Saint Nick - Sinter NiCOLAS - Sinter Colas (in Dutch): Santa Claus! And in the heat of the moment, as the heretic Arius made his argument that Jesus was not of the same nature as God himself, Nicholas walked over to him and punched him right in the face! So much for dignified theological debate.

The end product of the council was a statement of faith, based on Holy Scriptures, which clearly laid out what it meant to believe as a Christian. Using the Scriptures and an earlier simpler baptismal confession (the Apostles' Creed), Athanasius, the deacon from Egypt, crafted the document and it was signed by the bishops present. It was called the Nicene Creed. Some of the Arians refused to sign the document and were stripped of their offices. The Creed was copied and sent throughout the world as the first official document of the whole Church. Later (at the Council of Constantinople in 381) it was amended to include a statement about the Holy Spirit - that He too shared the divinity and substance of God the Father. It has, to this day, remained the quintessential definition of Christian belief.

Why Does It Matter to Us?

Some Christians today say, "But that is
old history and it doesn't matter to us now."
Some actually reject *any* creeds, saying, "No
Creed but Christ" (but that very statement in
itself *is* a creed, isn't it?). Some say, "We have
the Bible - that's all we need. We don't need
some man-made statement of faith," and then
they proceed to write their own man-made
statements of faith, failing to realize that the
same men who gave us the Creed gave us the
Canon of Scripture. A bit of historical data:
Our New Testament Canon was first listed by
the very same Athanasius, after he became a
bishop, in his Easter Letter of 367, and it was
universally confirmed at the Council of
Ephesus in 431. Think of it! For 431 years
there was *no* "New Testament" as we
understand it! And we received it from this
very company of bishops who gave us the
Creed. What I'm trying to show here is that
the Nicene Creed predates the Canon of the
New Testament by over 100 years! My point
is this: anyone who trusts in the authority of
the twenty seven books of the New Testament
(not, mind you, twenty five books, or thirty
books, but precisely these twenty seven) is
trusting in the Spirit-guided decisions of the
men who gave us the Creed. It is a serious
intellectual and theological flaw to accept one

(the New Testament) and to reject the other (the Creed).

For over fifteen hundred years the Nicene Creed has been the "symbol" of Christian belief. To believe it is to believe what Christians believe. To reject it is to reject what Christians believe.

We live in a time when many Christians don't know what they believe. Consequently they are open prey for any Scripture-twisting cult that comes along. David Koresh would never have made the newspapers if his followers had believed the Creed. Neither would Jim Jones. Or Joseph Smith. Or Mary Baker Eddy. Or Reverend Moon. Or...well, you get the point.

On the following pages we are going to study the two Creeds (Apostles' and Nicene) in order to strengthen ourselves in what it means to believe as true Christians. C.S. Lewis wrote a book entitled *Mere Christianity* in which he points out that among true Christians (Roman Catholics, Anglicans, Eastern Orthodox, Baptists, Methodist, Presbyterians, Pentecostals and a whole lot more) there is much more that unites us than divides us. But when we stand back and look at it, what unites us is the simple faith, the "mere" faith, of the Creeds. Using these documents as a framework, and turning to Scripture at every turn, we are going to "unpack" the suitcase of our faith and learn together what treasures we hold.

Chapter One

I Believe

Apostles' Creed:
"I believe..."

Nicene Creed:
"I believe..."

Both the Creeds, the Apostles' Creed (written sometime around A.D. 100) and the Nicene Creed (written in A.D. 325) begin with the words "I believe". In fact, our English word "creed" comes from *credo* - the first word of these statements of faith in Latin. The Apostles' Creed was originally (and still is) something said in the act of baptism. When a person is brought into the Christian faith through the waters of baptism the ceremony includes them being asked, "What do you believe?" And their response is, "*I believe* in God the Father Almighty..." The Nicene Creed, which is a fuller statement of Christian faith, was originally written by a group of bishops who were defending the faith against false teaching (see the Introduction), and was sent out to the worldwide Church to clarify and codify what it meant to believe like a Christian. In its original form it reads, "*We* believe..." because it was written from a group of leaders to the rest of the Church. But when it came to be repeated in the various churches the people quoted it by saying, "*I* believe". It was personal. Today, some churches say "I", and some churches say "We" and some churches, unfortunately, don't say anything at all. But in its original intent, just like the Apostles' Creed, it was meant to be personal..."I".

Taking it Personally

Being a Christian is a personal thing. I should point out that by personal I don't mean individual. Being a Christian is not an individual thing. When we become believers in Christ we also become members of his family, his Body, the Church. But as someone has said, "God has no grandchildren". Our relationship with him isn't mediated through some other channel so that we are *in* Christ but don't *know* Christ; real faith has a personal dimension to it. You can personally know God. You can personally pray to him. You can personally encounter his presence. You can personally obey him or disobey him. So, when the Creeds begin with "*I* believe" they mean just that. By personally affirming what the Church believes you are joining together with untold millions of Christians who throughout the ages have also embraced the truth of the Christian faith.

But - and this is a *big* but - what follows after the words "I believe" is not up to us. Although the Christian faith is personal, it isn't individualistic. You can't just make up your own creed (though heaven knows enough people have tried to). "I believe in peanut butter and jelly sandwiches" is not an accurate statement of what it means to be Christian! Our personal faith, our "I believe" joins with the whole of the Church in embracing the faith once delivered to the Apostles by Jesus himself.

How many times have you heard people say, when speaking of some text in the Bible, "Well, what it means to *me* is..."? Hopefully what they intend to say is, "Well, this is the *application* the text has for me." Application is one thing, interpretation is another. We approach the Bible, and the Christian faith, *together*. We don't believe whatever we want to believe. We believe what we have received from those who have gone before us. Saint Paul, writing the church in Corinth said, "For I *received* from the Lord what I also *passed on* to you: The Lord Jesus, on the night he was betrayed, took bread..." (1 Corinthians 11.23). The words that Paul used for *received* and *passed on* are technical words for the passing on of tradition. As Christians, we do the same. Like the Christians in Corinth, we receive the teachings of the Apostles, and we pass them on to those after us. So when we come to the words "I believe" in the Creeds, we should understand that we aren't making this stuff up as we go. We are standing at the end of a long line of men and women who have defended and protected the precious faith, some with their very lives, in order to pass it on to others. We believe the faith that has been delivered to us from the Prophets (the Old Testament), from Jesus, and from the Apostles (the New Testament), and which has been guarded and kept from their day until ours. What "*I* believe..." is of necessity what *we* believe.

What is Belief?

What, then, is belief? In our world, especially in our religious world, so impacted by the Enlightenment of the 17th century and afterward when everything turned to the mind and to theory, belief is usually seen as mental assent and nothing more. Mental assent *is* part of what it means to believe, but to believe something intellectually or with our mind is only the starting place of true faith. In the New Testament, when people cried out, "What must we do to be saved?", and the Apostles responded, "...believe on the Lord Jesus Christ..." (cf. Mark 16.16, Acts 16.31, Romans 10.9-10), they were not saying, "Well, all you have to do to be saved is to agree in your mind that Jesus was God come in the flesh, that he died and that he rose again. That's all you have to do and then you can get on with your life in just exactly the same way you've been living it all these years". The reason I know this is not what the Apostles meant is because the Apostles were Jewish. And Jews had a different understanding of belief than Greeks did.

For Jews there was no false separation between mental assent and fidelity, the two were a whole and one could not truly exist without the other. To believe something meant to embrace it with everything in you. If you believed something it *mattered*, and it had an impact on your whole life. When Jesus was asked what was the greatest commandment in the whole Old Testament, he responded by quoting Deuteronomy 6.4: "Love the Lord your God with all your heart and with all your soul and with all your mind" (Matthew 22.36). Did you notice the Jewish mindset? Jesus said, in effect, "Love God with everything in you." It is impossible to love God with our minds, and not with our heart and soul and body and strength. True believing impacts the whole person.

The Greek word for faith or belief (the New Testament was written in Greek, by the way) is *pistis*. Some etymologists (thats a twenty nine cent word for a person who studies where words come from) believe that *pistis* made its way into Latin as "pasta" and then Old French as "paste", meaning dough - that is, sticky stuff! In other words, they see our English word paste as having its roots in the Greek word for faith, *pistis*. Another way of saying "have faith" or "believe" is to say, "be glued to"! Whether that little word history is accurate or not, it certainly communicates the real idea behind believing. If I really believe something I'm going to be glued to it, not just in some mental way, but with my whole being.

The Bible tells us that "without faith [*pistis*; belief] it is impossible to please God, because anyone who comes to him must believe [*pistis*] that he exists and that he rewards those who earnestly seek him" (Hebrews 11.6). Belief, then, is necessary for salvation. And when we confess, "I believe..." we are saying, "With my whole being - body, soul and spirit - I embrace..."

What Do Christians Believe?

We come finally to the question, "What do Christians believe?" When my son Ken was in high school an extracurricular question emerged in a classroom when the students began discussing religion. They went around the room answering the question, "What does your church believe?" Some of the kids gave simple and uninformed answers, "Uh...well...we believe in Jesus". Others mis-answered the question by saying, "Well, we *don't* believe in dancing or drinking or smoking..." When it came Ken's turn he wasn't sure what he would say, but in one of those moments of sudden inspiration he remembered what he said every Sunday in church: "I believe in one God the Father Almighty, Maker of heaven and earth..." Before he could keep going another student across the room jumped up and said, "HEY! That's what *we* believe too!"

What do we believe? On the following pages you will find the text of both Creeds, side by side. Remember, the Apostles' Creed is the older basic baptismal creed. The Nicene is the fuller yet concise declaration of Christian faith.

Apostles' Creed	Nicene Creed
I believe in God the Father Almighty maker of heaven and earth;	I believe in one God, the Father Almighty maker of heaven and earth, And of all things visible and invisible;
And in Jesus Christ his only son our Lord;	And in one Lord Jesus Christ, the only-begotten Son of God; Begotten of his Father before all ages, God of God, Light of Light, True God of True God; Begotten, not made; Being of one substance with the Father; By whom all things were made. Who for us and for our salvation came down from heaven,
who was conceived by the Holy Spirit, born of the Virgin Mary,	And was incarnate by the Holy Spirit of the Virgin Mary, and was made man:

suffered under Pontius Pilate, was crucified, dead, and buried. He descended into hell.	And was crucified also for us under Pontius Pilate; He suffered death and was buried:
The third day he rose again from the dead. He ascended into heaven, and sits on the right hand of God the Father almighty. From there he shall come to judge the living and the dead.	And the third day he rose again according to the Scriptures: And ascended into heaven, And sits on the right hand of the Father: And he shall come again, with glory, to judge both the living and the dead; Whose kingdom shall have no end.
I believe in the Holy Spirit,	And I believe in the Holy Spirit, the Lord, and Giver of Life, Who proceeds from the Father and the Son; Who with the Father and the Son together is worshipped and glorified; Who spoke by the prophets.

the holy catholic Church, the communion of saints, the forgiveness of sins,	And I believe One, Holy, Catholic and Apostolic Church; I acknowledge one Baptism for the remission of sins;
the resurrection of the body, and the life everlasting. Amen.	And I look for the Resurrection of the dead, And the Life of the world to come. Amen.

Now that you have seen them side by side, let me share them with you in whole.

The Apostles' Creed

I believe in God, the Father almighty,
maker of heaven and earth;

And in Jesus Christ his only Son our Lord;
who was conceived by the Holy Spirit,
born of the Virgin Mary,
suffered under Pontius Pilate,
was crucified, dead, and buried.
He descended into hell.

The third day he rose again from the dead.
He ascended into heaven,

and sits on the right hand of God the Father almighty.
From there he shall come again to judge the living and the dead.

I believe in the Holy Spirit,
the holy catholic Church,
the communion of saints,
the forgiveness of sins,
the resurrection of the body,
and the life everlasting. Amen.

The Nicene Creed

I believe in one God, the Father Almighty
maker of heaven and earth,
And of all things visible and invisible;

And in one Lord Jesus Christ, the only-begotten
Son of God;
Begotten of his Father before all ages,
God of God, Light of Light, True God of True
God;
Begotten, not made;
Being of one substance with the Father;
By whom all things were made.
Who for us and for our salvation came down from
heaven,
And was incarnate by the Holy Spirit of the Virgin
Mary,
and was made man:

And was crucified also for us under Pontius Pilate;
He suffered death and was buried:
And the third day he rose again according to the
Scriptures:
And ascended into heaven,
And sits on the right hand of the Father:
And he shall come again, with glory, to judge both
the living and the dead;
Whose kingdom shall have no end.

And I believe in the Holy Spirit, the Lord, and
Giver of Life,
Who proceeds from the Father and the Son;
Who with the Father and the Son together is
worshipped and glorified;
Who spoke by the prophets.

And I believe One, Holy, Catholic and Apostolic
Church;
I acknowledge one Baptism for the remission of
sins;
And I look for the Resurrection of the dead,
And the Life of the world to come. Amen.

To believe this is to believe as a Christian. In
the following chapters we will explore each
segment of these Creeds, and we will discover
that each little phrase is full of wonderful truth
that brings us to God and brings us to
freedom.

Chapter Two

One God, The Father Almighty

The Apostles' Creed:
"I believe in God, the Father Almighty,
maker of heaven and earth."

The Nicene Creed:
"I believe in one God, the Father, the
Almighty, maker of heaven and earth,
and of all things visible and invisible."

To say "I believe in God" is the most
fundamental spiritual statement a human
being can make. It is a common statement that
can be made by all religions. Hindus, Muslims,
Jews, Christians, people who worship sticks
and stones as gods - all of them can and do
share the opening line of the Apostles' Creed:
"I believe in God..." This is the fundamental
statement that is the basis of religion itself. It

is also the starting place of the Christian religion, and hence the starting place of the Creeds. Everything else that will be said in the Creeds depends on this basic beginning. Everything else is an expansion, an unpacking, of this single line.

God is One

But the Creeds go on quickly to say more than just "I believe in God". They address precisely what God we believe in. And the first and most important thing to be said is that God is One.

Christians have looked for a single verse to capsulize the entire Gospel, and many have settled on John 3.16. This is the verse that many little Christian boys and girls memorize before they learn any other. In the Hebrew world of the Old Testament, every little Jewish boy and girl also had a first verse to memorize. It was understood to capsulize the whole of their faith, and it was the most important verse in the Bible. In fact, the context of the verse is a command from God through Moses that its content should be memorized, written down, posted on the walls, said before rising from bed and before closing the eyes to sleep. This verse is the epitome of what it means to be Jewish, as opposed to the pagans in the surrounding nations: "Hear, O Israel: The Lord our God, the Lord is one. Love the Lord your God with all your heart and with all your soul and with all your strength" (Deuteronomy 6.4-5)

When Jesus was asked what is the greatest commandment in the Bible, being a good and faithful Jew, he immediately quoted the verse he had memorized since his childhood: "Hear O Israel the Lord our God, the Lord is one..." (Mark 12.29). He went on to say that this verse was the fundamental basis for everything else in the Law and the Prophets. So the verse, called in Hebrew the *Schema*, is foundational not only for the Old Testament faith, but also for the Christian faith.

This idea of one God stands over against two pagan ideas, and you should remember that Judaism was an island of monotheism ("one God") in a sea of polytheism ("many gods").

The first pagan idea which belief in one God stands over against is *polytheism*, the idea that there is a plurality of gods. Idolaters, both ancient and modern, hold that there is a plethora of deities to which we pray and make petition. One god controls the rain, another orders the seasons, another gives strength in battle, another brings fertility to women. There were literally hundreds of gods, all requiring a sacrifice in order to answer a prayer. Often times (as in Greek and Roman mythology) these gods were somewhat scandalous beings epitomizing all the more base characteristics of humans themselves. Sometimes the gods were tricksters and deceivers; sometimes they were drunken sexual predators taking on human form and raping women; sometimes they were fierce in unjust battle and slaughtered innocent people. Almost always they carried some sense of arrogance and had to be appeased in various ways - including the extreme appeasement of human sacrifice. One neighboring nation of Israel worshipped a god named Molech whose chief sacrifice was newborn babies.

In contrast to this Israel stood up and proclaimed, "God is One"! There weren't a multitude of gods to be petitioned for various favors and appeased with various sacrifices; there was only one and he was unique, holy, and other. He was the God who had made everything and who was himself *unlike* everyone and everything else.

The second pagan idea that the *Schema* stands over against is *pantheism* - the idea that God is the *same* as creation. In other words, some pagans believed that all things are, in some way, God. The trees are God, the rivers are God, the animals are God, other people are God. Not, mind you, a multitude of gods, but that all things are part of God. There was, among these pagans, no distinction between the Creator and the created. In contrast, the Jews declared that God was wholly other. That everything else, and I mean *everything*, was made by him, but he was himself unmade. That everything else was finite - had a beginning and an end, but he was himself infinite. That everything else depended on him for its very existence, but he himself depended on no one or nothing. He simply was. He simply is. When Moses encountered God and asked him his name he simply said, "I AM" (Exodus 3.14).

It should be noted here, although it will be discussed more thoroughly in a later chapter, that there are not *three* Gods either. Tritheism, the notion of three Gods, is just another form of polytheism, that there are many Gods. The Christian revelation of the Holy Trinity - God as Father, Son and Holy Spirit is *not* a dividing of God into three beings. "Hear O Israel, the Lord our God, the Lord is *one*!"

The pantheists saw nature itself and everything in it as "God", and consequently lived in fear and subservience to nature itself. The Jews, on the other hand, understood God to be *above* nature (theologians call this *transcendence*) and consequently lived, not in fear of and subservience to nature, but in respect and love to the God who made nature, and who was able to move nature (that is, all creation) on their behalf according to his will.

The Father

Both the Old and New Testaments refer to this One True God as the Father. Sometimes in trying to communicate the nature of God the mistake is made of telling people, "Well, God is like your father..." But of course, some people have very bad father figures. Some fathers are abusive, some are absent, some are uncaring. To approach describing God in this fashion is to get the analogy backwards. Even those with the best of fathers have fathers with human flaws. The better application is that good fatherhood should be modeled on God, not that our understanding of God is modeled on good fatherhood.

Having said that, there is something inherent in our nature that tells us what a good father is like. A good father is loving. He is providing. He is protective. He is wise. These qualities are intuitively known to us because they are qualities possessed in and by God himself. These things are in the very nature of God.

To call God Father also implies that we are his children. On one level, all humanity is formed in his image, and he is the source of our being. On a deeper level, those who have a relationship with him - those who are in Christ - are uniquely his children and belong to his family. While the pagans lived in fear of the elements and the erratic nature of "the gods", Christians understand God to be a loving, providing, protective, wise, caring Father who watches over his children and is pleased to bless them with all the blessings he has to give. Saint Paul said it like this: "for he has blessed us in our union with Christ by giving us every spiritual gift in the heavenly world" (Ephesians 1.4; *An Australian Prayer Book* translation).

Almighty

That God is our Father is good and lovely, but if our Father in heaven is weak and limited (like the pagan gods) then we will not take full comfort in the simple fact of him being for us instead of against us. The Creeds go on to tell us that he is almighty. All mighty. Omni potent. Omnipotent.

Our Father in heaven loves us, cares for us, provides and protects us, and he is also completely able to do whatever he wishes to do. The prophet Jeremiah cried out, "Ah, Sovereign Lord, you have made the heavens and the earth by your great power and outstretched arm. *Nothing is too hard for you*" (Jeremiah 32.17), and Jesus said, "with God, *nothing is impossible*" (Luke 1.37). While the gods of the pagans were limited in power and influence (and hence there were many), the God of Christians is under the authority of no one else and is completely able within himself to accomplish his purposes in creation, in history, and in our own lives.

Some Christians need to redefine their perception of who God is. God is not an angry old man sitting in heaven peering down at us and just waiting for us to do something wrong so he can "smack" us. God is our all-powerful Father who loves us, is patient with us, and who literally gives himself so we can have fullness of life.

Maker of Heaven and Earth

Unlike the other "gods" who were themselves made, or were products of some "emanation" from a being above them, Christians serve a God who is himself the maker of *everything* else. How did he make all things? In the beginning he spoke creation into being by the power of his Word. Genesis tells us, "And God said, 'Let there be light,' and there was light" (1.3). In the Gospel of John we read, "In the beginning was the Word, and the Word was with God, and the Word was God. He was with God in the beginning. Through him all things were made; without him nothing was made that has been made" (1.1-3). Saint Paul writes, "For by him all things were created: things in heaven and on earth, visible and invisible, whether thrones or powers or rulers or authorities; all things were created by him and for him. He is before all things, and in him all things hold together" (Colossians 1.16-17).

We don't know the mechanics of creation; we don't know the details of the process. But we do know that God made everything that is not God. Let me say that again: God made everything that is not God! And if he made it, he owns it. All things belong to God: "The earth is the Lord's, and everything in it, the world, and all who live in it; for he founded it upon the seas and established it upon the waters" (Psalm 24.1-2).

We don't know the details of the "how" of creation, but we do know the "why". God did not create everything that exists out of some kind of necessity. God is complete in himself without need of anything else. He didn't *have* to make all that is. He did it out of his love and goodness. He did it to manifest his glory to that which is "other". To put it simply, knowing how good and delightful he himself was, he made everything else in order to *share himself* with it! He made creation, and he made you, to enjoy him!

The ancient Church Fathers saw one more reason he brought everything else into existence, and that was with an eye toward the incarnation. The Bible tells us (in John 1) that everything was made by the Word (who is God himself) and that the Word became flesh in the person of Jesus Christ. In the creation stories of Genesis the molding of humanity was the pinnacle of God's creation. In creating everything before mankind God simply spoke it into existence, but in his final act of creation he "got his hands dirty" and formed mankind *in his own image* (Genesis 1.27, 2.7). The early Church saw creation itself, and particularly the creation of humanity, as a vessel being prepared for God to inhabit. He was making a "house" for himself (all of creation) and in humanity he was creating the very point at which he would integrally join himself to his creation. This came to pass when, in the womb of the Virgin Mary, God made "a body for himself" - Jesus, who was himself, the pinnacle of all creation and the pinnacle of all humanity. The writer of Hebrews tells us, "Therefore, when Christ came into the world, he said: 'Sacrifice and offering you did not desire, but a body you prepared for me'" (Hebrews 10.5). Through the incarnation of Jesus Christ, and through the ongoing dwelling of the Holy Spirit in the members of the Church, God joined himself forever to his creation, and so all creation is made one with him and can truly love and enjoy him forever.

Visible and Invisible

When the Nicene Creed states that God made "all things, visible and invisible" it divides creation into two parts.

The visible is the physical. Everything that can be seen. As science progresses we can see more and more. We can see the minutest particles and we can see the distant stars and galaxies. God made it all.

The invisible is the spiritual realm -
heaven, the angels and archangels, the
cherubim and seraphim who continually praise
God around his throne. Oftentimes when we
think of creation we think only of the seen -
the mountains and trees and rivers and
streams, the animals and humanity. We might
be tempted to think of the "other realm" the
invisible world, as somehow "uncreated". But
this realm too is part of creation, part of
nature. This is why, throughout the Bible,
when men are tempted to worship some angel
of God, the angel is quick to say, "Don't
worship me" - as if to say, "I am a creature too,
just like you. Only the Uncreated One is to be
worshipped". It is erroneous for us to call the
invisible heavenly world the "supernatural" It
too is natural. It too is part of God's creation.
It too was made to love God and to enjoy him
forever.

In the creation of humanity we find a
connection between the visible and invisible.
We are members of the physical world, having
skin and bones and blood and muscles and
being made of the stuff of the earth. We are
also members of the spiritual world, having
God's breath breathed into us from the
beginning, and being made spirits like the
heavenly beings.

Implications

All this is not simply boring and empty
theology. Truth always has implications in our
real lives. If God is the maker of all (and he
is), and if he has made all things to know, love
and enjoy himself (and he has), then in order
to fully become ourselves we must give
ourselves to knowing and serving our Creator.
Nothing exists which does not owe its
existence to God. Everything from amoebae
and earthworms to angels and archangels were
created by God with purpose and destiny. And
that purpose and destiny are wrapped up in
the person of the One True God. We are his
and he is ours and the relationship between
God and all creation is one of love.

Chapter Three

Jesus Christ...Conceived by the Holy Spirit...Born of the Virgin Mary

The Apostles' Creed:
"And in Jesus Christ his only Son our Lord;
who was conceived by the Holy Spirit, born of
the Virgin Mary."

The Nicene Creed:
"And in one Lord Jesus Christ,
the only begotten Son of God;
begotten of his Father before all ages,
God of God, Light of Light, True God of True
God; begotten, not made;
being of one substance with the Father;
by whom all things were made: who for us and
for our salvation came down from heaven,
And was incarnate by the Holy Spirit
of the Virgin Mary,
And was made man."

The knock on my door came in the middle of the afternoon. Two nicely dressed young men in white shirts and dark ties asked if they could come in and talk to me about Jesus. They were riding bicycles. Theologically speaking, I had both barrels loaded. We met for several weeks, once a week, and I pretended to be a novice with lots of questions. But I had special questions that threw them into disarray. Toward the end of our sessions, one of them was transferred away, and I later learned that this was standard operating procedures when one of their missionaries began to doubt what they were espousing.

The various cults which lay claim to the name "Christian" usually share one thing in common: they reject that Jesus Christ is God come in the flesh. But they are tricky. They will say, "I believe that Jesus is the Son of God." And it all sounds so good. But when you put them on the spot and reply, "Well, that's just wonderful! Let me ask you, do you believe that Jesus Christ is God the Son?", they will almost always backpedal and confess that this is *not* what they believe. Do you notice the subtle difference? To say that Jesus Christ is the Son of God can mean almost anything. On some level Adam was a son of

God. Kings are called "sons of God" in the Old Testament. So are angels. But to say that Jesus Christ is God the Son is an entirely different statement. It is saying that Jesus *is* God, pure and simply. Not that he is *from* God or he is *like* God but that he *is* God.

The heresies of our own day are not new. They have been around for a long time. Arius (remember the Saint Nicholas story in the Introduction?) was a 4th century heretic who said he believed the Apostles' Creed: "I believe in Jesus Christ his only Son our Lord...". But he adamantly refused to say that Jesus was God the Son. Hence the Council of Nicea in A.D. 325, and hence the full definition of who Jesus is that we find in the Nicene Creed.

The first clause of the Creeds addresses the reality of God the Father. There is one God, period. He made everything and upholds everything by his power. The second clause turns our attention to the person of God the Son.

Our Lord

The opening statement about Jesus in the Apostles' Creed seems to say it all, and

59

most Christians would understand it to say that Jesus is God come in the flesh. But Arius and other early heretics claimed to be able to agree with the creedal statement while not embracing the deity of Christ. Here, then, are some ways they could read it:

"...His only Son our Lord" - Jesus is *our* Lord, *our* master, but there are many ways to God. Others have other Lords. So while we see Jesus as our pathway to God and we follow his teachings, others may see Siddhartha Gautama (the original Buddha) as their master who points them to the way of everlasting life (or everlasting non-existence, as the case may be). Or they may see someone like Reverend Moon as a *new* messenger from God, or Joseph Smith as someone who brings to the table *additional* information about how we follow God.

"Jesus was mortal." He was just a man. Special, yes, but still a mortal. Maybe not a "mere" mortal, but a mortal. The cultists of past and present will even concede that he was miraculously born of a virgin (with which, oddly enough, Muslims agree), but he is still made of *only* the same stuff we are all made of - humanity. They see him as unique in that God has specially chosen him, and he is therefore called the (or "a") Son of God, but he isn't God himself.

Some of the heretics actually took the opposite tack - that Jesus is truly God, but he didn't *really* become a man. He only *appeared* to be a man; he was God dressing up in human form for thirty three years, but on the cross the deity departed from the human body and Jesus died as a mere mortal.

All these false teachings completely missed out on the deeper meaning of the word *Lord*. This next bit is a little technical, but it is very important. When God revealed his name to Moses (in Exodus 3.14) he said he was "I AM"; "I BE"; "I EXIST". It was a huge statement in a few words. God declared that he simply IS. He has no beginning and no end. He depends on nothing else for his being. Everything else is made, he is the Unmade. We call ourselves human *beings*, but we aren't, really. We are human *becomings* - we are always changing, growing, modifying, dying. Unlike us (or anything else in creation) God "BEs". He IS.

So when God gave his name as "I AM" it became a sacred name. The Jews thought it so sacred that they refused to write the whole word and left out the vowels, leaving only the consonants: Y...H...W...H. Nowadays no one even knows what the vowels were, so different Bible translations put different letters in between the consonants: YeHoWaH: "Jehovah" or YaHWeH: "Yahweh". When it came to saying the name of God it was considered unpronounceable, so the Jews substituted the word *Adonai*, that is "Lord". Even today in many English translation you will read about the LORD God. Notice that the word LORD is in all capitals; this is a way to signify in English the sacred name of God.

When the Old Testament was first translated into Greek (in 300 B.C.) the translators translated *Adonia* using the Greek word *kurios*, which means lord or master or governor. Later, when the Apostles wrote the New Testament in Greek, they also used the word *kurios* or *Lord* in reference to Jesus. But they weren't saying that Jesus was simply a master, or a governor. They were saying that Jesus was *Adonia*. That Jesus was Jehovah. That Jesus was Yahweh. That Jesus was *one and the same* with God!

When doubting Thomas, who missed out on seeing the risen Jesus with the rest of the Apostles, finally encountered him, he put his fingers into the wounds of Jesus and declared, "My *Lord* and my *God*" (John

20.28)! When Saint Stephen was being stoned to death, he cried out, "*Lord* Jesus receive my spirit" (Acts 7.59). When the disciples baptized people into the Christian faith they baptized them in "the name of the *Lord* Jesus" (Acts 8.16). The declaration repeatedly made by the Apostles throughout the book of Acts was regarding "the *Lord* Jesus" (9.17, 10.36, 11.20, 15.11, 15.26, 20.21, 28.31). When Paul told people how to be saved he said, "Believe in the *Lord* Jesus and you will be saved..." (Acts 16.31). When Saint Paul wrote about Jesus he said things like:

> •"If you confess with your mouth, "Jesus is *Lord*," and believe in your heart that God raised him from the dead, you will be saved" (Romans 10.9).
> •"The God of peace will soon crush Satan under your feet. The grace of our *Lord* Jesus be with you" (Romans 16.20).
> •"To the church of God in Corinth, to those sanctified in Christ Jesus and called to be holy, together with all those everywhere who call on the name of our *Lord* Jesus Christ—their *Lord* and ours" (1 Corinthians 1.2).
> •"There is but one *Lord*, Jesus Christ, through whom all things came and

through whom we live" (1 Corinthians 6.8).

The title "Lord Jesus" is used 101 times in the New Testament. It is a magnificent declaration that Jesus is the One who made all things, and who has now come among us, born of a Virgin. But none of this mattered to the false teachers, and so two hundred years after the Apostles' Creed was formed, the Nicene Creed expanded on the idea, and left no wiggle room for heretics.

Begotten of His Father Before All Ages

Most people see the word "begotten" and automatically think "born". But begotten doesn't mean born. Birthing is something that happens from the female gender. Begetting is something that happens from the male gender. It takes two - the male begets - that is, he gives his seed, and the female births - that is, she brings forth. When the Bible says that Jesus is "the only begotten Son" it is not in any way a reference to what happened with the Virgin Mary or with his birth. It is a statement of his relationship to God. The Hebrew word literally means "brought forth" or "published". God the Son wasn't begotten in Bethlehem! He was begotten, as the Creed says, "eternally". Eternally means forever - past, present and future, outside time. God the Son has *always* been "published" or "brought forth" by the God the Father. The prophet Micah used the same word when he prophesied that the Messiah would be born in Bethlehem, he wrote, "But you, Bethlehem Ephrathah, though you are small among the clans of Judah, out of you will come for me one who will be ruler over Israel, whose *origins* (other translations say "*generations*" or "*goings forth*") are from of old, from ancient times (or "from days of eternity")" (Micah 5.2). There never was a time when he wasn't begotten. The "begottenness" of God the Son did not begin at creation, nor at his birth as a man. He was begotten "before all ages" - before time - eternally. He was not begotten at a point in time, or even at a point before time (a logical impossibility). He was, is and will be always "being brought forth" from the Father.

He is indeed the *only* manifestation of the Father - the "*only begotten* Son" - so that when God is seen, heard, touched - wherever and whenever God is encountered at all - it is proper to understand this as the Son showing forth the invisible "interior" God - the Father (cf. John 1.1,14,18, 6.46, 14.7-9).

God from God...
One Substance with the Father

The Son is not another "entity" from
the Father. There are not two Gods (or three).
The Son is not someone or something "other
than" the Father. The Creed establishes the
Scriptural teaching that the Son is "God from
God...true God from true God". The emphasis
here is on the union of the Father and Son,
and this idea culminates with the overarching
phrase, "being of one substance with the
Father". There is only one substance, one
"stuff" of God, and it is God himself. Deity
isn't spread around throughout the universe.
God is omnipresent (in all places - this doesn't
mean that God is so *big* that he fills up
everywhere, it means that God is fully and
totally everywhere at once. All of God is here
and all of God is there, he fills all in all). There
are not batches of divinity parceled out. There
is simply the stuff of God, the substance of
God, and it is one because *he* is One.

When the Creed proclaims that the Son
is "of one substance with the Father" it means
there is no division between them. In these
short words we find a reaffirmation of the
Schema in Deuteronomy 6.4: "Hear O Israel
the Lord our God, the Lord is one". God the

Son is the manifestation of that One God, whether that happened in the Old Testament (creation, God's appearances to Moses and others, etc.) or the New Testament, when "the Word was God...[and] the Word became flesh" (John 1.1-14).[1]

By Whom All Things Were Made

Just to make sure they weren't misunderstood, the writers of the Nicene Creed went on to say that it was the Son who made everything. We have seen in the first clause of both Creeds that God the Father is the maker of heaven and earth. Now we are told that God the Father (that invisible, unseeable, untouchable, inner reality of God that dwells in light unaccessible - cf. Exodus 33.20, Judges 13.22, Matthew 6.6, 18, John 1.18, 6.46, 1 Timothy 6.16) has created all things *by* and *through* God the Son - God made manifest.

The Incarnation

We now come to the central truth of Christianity: "Who for us and for our salvation came down from heaven". God the Son, the

---

[1] For a full statement of how the early Church addressed these matters, see Appendix One: The Athanasian Creed.

very manifestation of the invisible God himself, the one who is the Word of God and brought all things into existence, the one who revealed himself to Moses and Joshua and the Prophets, "came down from heaven". And his coming from the heavenly dimension into our realm of the physical was not just for a visit, but for an eternal union with what he had made, and in particular with humanity. But it must be emphasized that this wonderful act was not for himself - he didn't "need" to join himself to us - he did it for "us and for our salvation". The very act of the incarnation ("enfleshing") was to save creation and restore mankind to himself. It was an act of love.

How he came down from heaven was that he became "incarnate by the Holy Spirit of the Virgin Mary". In the third and final clause of the creeds we will learn more of the Holy Spirit, but here we see the Spirit of God is referenced as that life, that energy, that "flow" between the Father and the Son, and it was by the Spirit that the Son became flesh. The angel Gabriel appeared to the Virgin Mary and told her, "The Holy Spirit will come upon you, and the power of the Most High will overshadow you. So the holy one to be born will be called the Son of God" (Luke 1.35).

And thus, for us, was God "made man".
In the womb of the Virgin Mary God joined
himself to his creation. He took the flesh of
Mary - her egg, and joined himself to her flesh
and the child born was without human father
but was of human mother. "The Word became
flesh" (John 1.14). In the early Church the
Virgin was given the title, "Mary, Mother of
God". Some people have been thrown off by
this title, feeling that it elevated Mary to too
high an honor. Laying aside for a moment that
the Bible actually says that all generations will
call her Blessed and that she is blessed among
all women(Luke 1.42, 48), the title is not
about Mary, but about Jesus. The title is not a
marian statement, but a christological
statement. It is saying that what was in the
womb of Mary was really and truly God, "true
God of true God"! In the inner chamber of
humanity, in the womb of the Virgin Mary,
God became man. He did not simply put on a
human costume. He became man. Never again
to *not* be man! God elevated the stuff of our
nature to the place of Divinity eternally! Jesus
Christ is *fully* God and *fully* man and the two
shall nevermore be divided or separated. A
man - one of us - sits enthroned in the
heavenlies *forever* and is God Almighty! And it
was all an act of love, a reuniting, a
reconciling: "God was in Christ Jesus,

69

reconciling the world to himself, not counting men's sins against them" (2 Corinthians 5.19)!

Chapter Four

He was Crucified, Dead and Buried

The Apostles' Creed:
"He suffered under Pontius Pilate, was crucified, dead and buried."

The Nicene Creed:
"And was crucified also for us under Pontius Pilate; He suffered death and was buried."

It is interesting that both Creeds, having announced the birth of Jesus Christ, skip right over thirty three years of his life, including all his teachings and miracles, and focus in on the final few days: his suffering, death and burial.

The reason for this is that all Jesus' teachings and miracles were predecessors -

indeed, were signs and instructions - pointing to and relating to his death and resurrection. It was for this purpose that he came into the world. What he accomplished in these few days is what he came to accomplish. This is why his ministry could be summed up by John the Baptist in these few words: "Behold, the Lamb of God, who takes away the sins of the world" (John 19.30). He was the sacrificial lamb that brought forgiveness of sins for the whole world by the sacrifice of himself.

He Suffered Under Pontius Pilate

Other than Jesus himself, and his mother the Virgin Mary, no one else is named in the creeds except the Roman governor Pontius Pilate. By mentioning his name, the creeds firmly connect the story of our salvation (and the salvation of the world) to datable time and history.

Pontius Pilate was the Roman Procurator of Judea from A.D. 26 to 36. For ten years he was involved in all the political intrigue associated with the Roman Empire, and he showed himself to be the kind of politician that gives politicians a bad name - more concerned with expediency than justice or honesty.

The odd thing is that Pilate absolved himself of the whole matter of Jesus' crucifixion. Giving in to the desires of the religious/political leaders of the day, he allowed Jesus to be beaten and mocked, but his intention was not to have him crucified. After questioning Jesus and finding no fault in him, instead of standing up for him, Pilate simply walked away from the whole matter: "When Pilate saw that he was getting nowhere, but that instead an uproar was starting, he took water and washed his hands in front of the crowd. 'I am innocent of this man's blood,' he said. 'It is your responsibility!'" (Matthew 27.24). Sadly, this action not only made way for the death of Jesus, but it forever earned infamy for Pilate, who would henceforth be remembered as a coward more concerned with his own popularity than with justice.

He Suffered and was Crucified

Having said that Jesus suffered under Pontius Pilate, we should not lay the responsibility for his suffering and death fully on Pilate's shoulders. To whom, then, should the blame be given? In the past some have erroneously said that the Jews were responsible for the death of Jesus. An unfortunate (and long) episode in Church history is the evil treatment which Jews have received at the hands of Christians for "their" killing of the Messiah. Indeed the Jewish leadership called for his death, and the crowds (the same crowds, by the way, who only days before had praised him as the "Son of David") did add their consent to Jesus' death by shouting "Crucify him!" But it is not on the shoulders of the Jewish people that guilt should be laid.

Others have laid the blame at the feet of the Romans. After all, it was only by the consent of the Roman authorities that a death penalty could be carried out. And although it was the High Priest and religious leaders who called for his execution, it was, in the end, Roman soldiers who actually did the deed. But the blame for the death of Jesus doesn't rest with the Romans either.

Who then is responsible for this catastrophe, this killing of an innocent man, this most heinous of all heinous crimes, executing God who came in the flesh? The prophet Isaiah, foreseeing these events, clearly places the blame where it belongs: "He was despised and rejected by men, a man of sorrows, and familiar with suffering. Like one from whom men hide their faces he was despised, and we esteemed him not. Surely he took up our infirmities and carried our sorrows, yet we considered him stricken by God, smitten by him, and afflicted. But he was pierced for our transgressions, he was crushed for our iniquities; the punishment that brought us peace was upon him, and by his wounds we are healed. We all, like sheep, have gone astray, each of us has turned to his own way; and the Lord has laid on him the iniquity of us all" (Isaiah 53.3-6).

He took up *our* infirmities. He carried *our* sorrows. He was pierced for *our* transgressions. He was crushed for *our* iniquities. The punishment that brought *us* peace was upon him. *We all*, like sheep, have gone astray. The Lord laid upon him the iniquity of *us all*. In the final analysis the fault might be traced back to Adam himself, through whom sin entered the world (Romans 5.12). But we are all sons and daughters of Adam, and we are all sinners, and there is none righteous, no not one (Romans 3.10). Who is to blame for what happened on that hill outside Jerusalem? I am. You are. We all are.

Nor was what happened that day an accident. All throughout the ministry of Jesus his own disciples didn't "get it". At first, like everyone else, they were expecting the Messiah to be a political/military leader who would free Israel from the chains of Rome. When Jesus talked about his approaching death they were confused. Even Peter, to whom it had been revealed that this Jesus was "the Christ, the Son of the Living God" (Matthew 16.16) rebuked Jesus when he talked of his looming death: "Peter took him aside and began to rebuke him. 'Never, Lord!' he said. 'This shall never happen to you!' Jesus turned and said to Peter, 'Get behind me, Satan! You are a stumbling block to me; you do not have in mind the things of God, but the things of men'" (Matthew 16.22-23). Even though they had all the writings of the Prophets, they couldn't wrap their minds around the idea that Jesus had actually come into this world to do away with sin *by the offering of himself*!

Jesus wasn't what anyone expected in a Messiah. He had come to show that the way of the cross was the way of life. What happened that dark spring day on the hill of Golgotha was, ultimately, not the doing of Pilate, or the Jews, or the Romans, or even all of us. It was the work of God himself: "Yet it was the *Lord's will* to crush him and cause him to suffer, and though the LORD makes his life a guilt offering" (Isaiah 53.10). Jesus' death was, according to Peter, by "the definite plan and foreknowledge of God" (Acts 2.23). Jesus said, "The reason my Father loves me is that I lay down my life - only to take it up again. *No one takes it from me, but I lay it down of my own accord.* I have authority to lay it down and authority to take it up again. This command I received from my Father" (John 10.17-18). Later, John the Beloved would write, "This is how we know what love is: *Jesus Christ laid down his life* for us" (1 John 3.16).

Some Christians who misunderstand the Trinity and think of God as a kind of "corporation" of three distinct beings (which is really tritheism, not trinitarianism) have a hard time imagining a father sacrificing a son. No good and loving father would sacrifice a son when he could sacrifice himself! But a proper understanding of the Godhead (see the previous chapter) makes it clear: God gave himself! If Jesus is God come in the flesh - God the One and Only taking on flesh - then it was an action of great *self-sacrifice* that led to the cross! The One who is Life himself took on death for us. The one who *made* the wood of the cross and the iron of the nails willingly laid himself down on that wood to have those nails driven through his hands and feet!

And to what end? To deal *once* and *for all* (for *all* time and for *all* people and for *all* creation) with the sin that separated fallen man and fallen creation from the Maker: "The death he died, he died to sin *once for all*; but the life he lives, he lives to God" (Romans 6.10). The writer of Hebrews expands on what Saint Paul said: "Such a high priest meets our need - one who is holy, blameless, pure, set apart from sinners, exalted above the heavens. Unlike the other high priests, he does not need to offer sacrifices day after day, first for his own sins, and then for the sins of the people. He sacrificed for their sins *once for all* when *he offered himself*" (Hebrew 7.26-27), and again, "But now he has appeared *once for all* at the end of the ages to do away with sin by *the sacrifice of himself*" (Hebrews 9.26).

Through the sacrifice of himself, Jesus ensured that the whole world stood reconciled to God (2 Corinthians 5.19)! What happened on the cross that day was the beginning of "the great reversal". From that time forward the way to God was cleared of all obstacles and free passage was given to everyone. This is *not* some kind of cheap universalism, but it *is* (as Lutheran theologians call it) "universal justification". God, in Christ, did the necessary work of creating a union between humanity and God that is freely given to every person -

"Salvation is found in no one else, for there is no other name under heaven given to men by which we must be saved" (Acts 4.12).

Dead and Buried

When the Creeds say that Jesus was "dead" or "suffered death" they mean that he really and truly died. He was dead. Really dead. Not just sort of dead. Not just a little bit dead. Dead dead. Not swooning. Not pretending to be dead. Not dead in some way different than the dead all humans experience. When Jesus breathed his last breath on the cross he was as dead as a human being can be. But in that very death he struck the death knell for death itself! His death was the first step in the accomplishment of the defeat of death and salvation from death for us all.

The Creeds also make a point to say that Jesus was buried. Jesus' body was laid in a tomb as a dead body. In other words, as Saint Gregory of Nyssa wrote, "at Christ's death his soul was separated from his flesh" (Great Catechism, chapter 16).

Being crucified on a Friday, lying in the tomb was a kind of "Sabbath rest" for Jesus, and a foreshadowing of the rest that comes for us all in the culmination of all things in the new creation of heaven and earth (Hebrews 4.1-10).

  We are told that Jesus was buried in the borrowed tomb of Joseph of Arimathea: "Now there was a man named Joseph, a member of the Council, a good and upright man, who had not consented to their decision and action. He came from the Judean town of Arimathea and he was waiting for the kingdom of God. Going to Pilate, he asked for Jesus' body. Then he took it down, wrapped it in linen cloth and placed it in a tomb cut in the rock, one in which no one had yet been laid. It was Preparation Day, and the Sabbath was about to begin" (Luke 23.50-54). This is a telling incident, for it hints at the fact that the tomb was only borrowed! As someone has humorously said, "He only needed it for the weekend!" The Scriptures promised that Jesus' body would not see decay. Prophetically seeing this great day, King David wrote, "Therefore my heart is glad and my tongue rejoices; my body also will rest secure, because you will not abandon me to the grave, nor will you let your Holy One see decay." (Psalm 16.9-10). In Peter's first great sermon, on the Day of Pentecost, he expanded on what David had said: "Men of Israel, listen to this: Jesus of Nazareth was a man accredited by God to you by miracles, wonders and signs, which God did among you through him, as you yourselves know. This man was handed over to you by God's set purpose and foreknowledge; and you, with the help of wicked men, put him to death by nailing him to the cross. But God raised him from the dead, freeing him from the agony of death, because it was impossible for death to keep its hold on him. David said about him: 'I saw the Lord always before me. Because he is at my right hand, I will not be shaken. Therefore my heart is glad and my tongue rejoices my body also will live in hope, because you will not abandon me to the grave, nor will you let your Holy One see decay. You have made known to me the paths of life; you will fill me with joy in your presence.' Brothers, I can tell you confidently that the patriarch David died and was buried, and his tomb is here to this day. But he was a prophet and knew that God had promised him on oath that he would place one of his descendants on his throne. Seeing what was ahead, he spoke of the resurrection of the Christ, that he was not abandoned to the grave, nor did his body see decay. God has raised this Jesus to life, and we are all witnesses of the fact. Exalted to the right hand of God, he has received from the Father the promised Holy Spirit and has poured out what you now see and hear" (Acts 2.26-33).

Jesus really died and he was really buried as a dead man. But, as Peter said in his sermon, "It was impossible for death to keep its hold on him" (v. 24)!

Chapter Five

He Descended Into Hell

The Apostles' Creed:
"He descended into hell."

This little phrase in the middle of the Apostles' Creed isn't even found in the Nicene Creed and is one of the most overlooked and at the same time most exciting lines in all theology. Jesus went to hell? Whatever could that mean?

First, it follows on the heels of the phrase, "He was crucified, dead and buried." With four short words this little sentence describes what happened in the life and ministry of Christ during his entombment. Here is the story of what happened *between* the death and resurrection of Jesus!

He Descended Into Hell As A Dead Man

We have already seen that Jesus died a
sinner's death, exchanging his sinlessness for
our sins and taking upon himself the sins of us
all. Saint Paul wrote, "God made him who had
no sin to be sin for us, so that in him we might
become the righteousness of God" (2
Corinthians 5.21). A sinner's death includes
not only physical death, but a kind of spiritual
death - a descent into hell (Greek: *hades*, the
abode of the dead). In other words, Jesus was
suffering the consequences of the fall of Adam:
death; death as a human.

One of the things Jesus cried out on the
cross (he was actually quoting Psalm 22 from
the cross) was, "My God, my God, why have
you forsaken me?" (Matthew 27.46). In the
deep agony of the cross, Jesus was somehow
experiencing being forsaken by God. This is a
tearing at the very fabric of his being, a
descending to the lowest dimension of human
existence - death and the place of the dead,
hell, or hades. And so, to begin with, the
descent into hell can be seen as part of Christ's
humiliation - his passion. But more properly, it
is seen (and we shall come to this
momentarily) as a part of his exaltation.
Christ's descent into hell is the nadir - the

lowest point - of his humiliation, and it is also the beginning of the reversal of all things when he is exalted as King of Kings and Lord of Lords.

He Descended Into Hell as a Missionary

When the Apostle Peter writes of this moment he tells us, "He was put to death in the body but made alive by the Spirit, through whom also he went and preached to the spirits in prison who disobeyed long ago when God waited patiently in the days of Noah while the ark was being built" (1 Peter 3.18-20). Later in the same epistle Peter wrote, "For this is the reason the gospel was preached even to those who are now dead, so that they might be judged according to men in regard to the body, but live according to God in regard to the spirit" (4.6).

Jesus descended into hell, not only as a human, but as the victorious Lord, and part of what he did was *preach*! There has been much discussion as to what Jesus preached. Some see his "preaching" as a kind of "I told you so" to all the souls in hell. I would suggest that Jesus preached the same thing he preached everywhere: the announcement of the arrival of the Kingdom of God and the declaration of reconciliation through his sacrifice. Hell was the place that more than anywhere else showed man's terrible state of separation from God. Hades, the abode of the dead, is where all the dead were - righteous Moses and David, the godly Prophets, but also those who had lived a life of separation from God. Now, while his body lay in the tomb, Jesus descended into the lower regions and proclaimed salvation to everyone who was separated from God and his life.

He Descended Into Hell As A Victor

My favorite icon (those ancient pictures which Christians in the Orthodox East use as instruments of worship) is called "The Harrowing of Hell". It depicts Jesus coming out of the tomb - not gently, but *leaping*, his robe fluttering behind him in the wind almost like a kind of Superman's cape! Scattered all around him are the broken down doors, the shattered wood, and the broken locks and hinges of hell itself. With one hand he is grasping Adam and with another he is holding on to Eve, and a whole crew of people are scurrying out behind him. He has just conquered hell and freed its captives.

When the Apostle John was in exile on the Isle of Patmos he had a vision of the risen Lord who told him, "I am the Living One; I was dead, and behold I am alive for ever and ever! And I hold the keys of death and Hades" (Revelation 1.18). From whence did he *get* those keys? Well, he got them from death and hell and the grave - when he descended there in his own death. While he was in hell he not only experienced the depths of human death, he not only preached to those who were there, he also conquered the evil powers! Paul writes, "And having *disarmed the powers and authorities*, he made a public spectacle of them, triumphing over them by the cross" (Colossians 2.15).

Before he died Jesus told the Pharisees that they would see "the sign of Jonah": "Then some of the Pharisees and teachers of the law said to him, 'Teacher, we want to see a miraculous sign from you.' He answered, 'A wicked and adulterous generation asks for a miraculous sign! But none will be given it except the sign of the prophet Jonah. For as Jonah was three days and three nights in the belly of a huge fish, so the Son of Man will be three days and three nights in the heart of the earth'"(Matthew 12.38-40). Jesus being in the grave for three days is related to Jonah being in the belly of the beast for three days. But on the third day Jonah was spat out by the beast! Jesus was in the belly of hell for three days, but on the third day hell could not keep its grip on him and gave him up!

The early Church Fathers have seen this descent into hell as a fulfillment of Job 40.1, where God asks Job, "Who can capture with a hook the great sea monster Leviathan [the Dragon]?" In his descent into hell, as a human, Jesus "tricked" the trickster, the devil, that old serpent, the dragon. Saint Cyprian wrote, "The divine power of God's son was a kind of fishhook hidden by the covering of human flesh".[2] Saint Gregory of Nyssa wrote, "...the deceiver reaps the harvest of the seeds he sowed with his own free will. For he who first deceived man by the bait of pleasure is himself deceived by the camouflage of human nature..."! John of Damascus explained it like this: "Wherefore death approaches, and swallowing up the body as a bait is transfixed on the hook of divinity, and after tasting of the sinless and life-giving body, perishes, and brings up again all whom of old he swallowed up. For just as darkness disappears on the introduction of light, so is death repulsed before the assault of life, and brings life to all, but death to the destroyer".

---

[2] For this and the following quotes, see Thomas Oden, *The Word of Life*, 1989, Peabody, MA, Hendrickson Press, pp. 400, 443).

Do you see the brilliance of this strategic move? Satan rejoices in the death of Jesus, and the demons of hell celebrate his descent into *their* territory! But the shouts of joy soon turn to howls of terror when they realize that the One among them is himself Life and Light that cannot be extinguished! To put it another way, hell's gates are broken down *from the inside out*! The great reversal has begun.

Back to "the sign of Jonah". Saint Cyril of Jerusalem wrote, "Jonah was cast into the belly of a great fish, but Christ of His own will descended to the abode of the invisible fish of death. he went down of His own will to make death disgorge those it had swallowed up, according to the Scripture: 'I shall deliver them from the power of the nether world, and I shall redeem them from death.' (Hosea 13.14). His body, therefore, was made a bait to death, that the dragon, when hoping to devour it, might disgorge those whom he had already devoured."

Finally, a line from Saint Bonaventure: Christ "tore the prey away from him, broke down the gates of hell and bound the serpent. Disarming the Principalities and Powers, he led them away boldly, displaying them openly in triumph in himself (Col. 2.15). Then the Leviathan was led about with a hook (Job 40.25), his jaw pierced by Christ so that he who had no right over the Head which he had attacked, also lost what he had seemed to have over the body."

When Paul wrote about this momentous occasion he quoted Psalm 68.18 and said, "This is why it says: 'When he ascended on high, he led captives in his train and gave gifts to men.' What does 'he ascended' mean except that he also *descended to the lower, earthly regions*?" (Ephesians 4.7-9).

Christ's descent into hell was an action of extending his lordship to the furthest dimension of human experience and to the furthest dimension of creation. Paul said, "Therefore God exalted him to the highest place and gave him the name that is above every name, that at the name of Jesus every knee should bow, in heaven and on earth and *under the earth*, and every tongue confess that Jesus Christ is Lord, to the glory of God the Father" (Philippians 2.9-11).

A movement that began at the nadir - the lowest point of descent - turns suddenly to the beginning of an ascension back into glory and authority and power. Here, in the darkness of hell, the mighty triumph of Christ is underway. And all this happens just before the next line of the creeds: "On the third day he rose again from the dead"!

Chapter Six

The Third Day He Rose Again

The Apostles' Creed:
"The third day he rose again from the dead."

The Nicene Creed:
"And the third day he rose again according to
the Scriptures."

Now we come to the core belief of the
Christian faith. Without it none of the other
doctrines matter. Without it, the life, ministry,
teachings and death of Christ are meaningless.
"If Christ be not raised," Saint Paul wrote,
"our preaching is in vain" (1 Corinthians
15.14). The resurrection of Jesus Christ from
the dead is the lynchpin of Christianity - "Of
first importance," Paul writes (1 Corinthians
15.3).

Only one Gospel records the details of the birth of Jesus. His teachings and miracles are variously covered by different Gospels, some leaving out what others contain. But the resurrection of Jesus is recorded in all four gospels, and in the epistles of the Apostles, and is central to their message.

The Third Day He Rose Again

The Romans called the first day of the week "The Day of the Sun". The rest of the days were also named after the heavenly bodies. In English it remains the same: Sun Day, Moon Day, Tyr's Day (Nordic for Mars), Woden's Day (Mercury), Thor's Day (Jupiter), Friden's Day (Venus) and Saturn's Day. Oddly, Sunday has remained, in the English language, named after the star around which our planet revolves. In Spanish and Portuguese the days are named after the planets and the old gods too. Except for one. Speakers of those languages call the first day of the week Domingo - the day of the Dom - the Day of the Lord.

Jesus was buried on a Friday. The second day, the Sabbath (our Saturday) his body was in the tomb and his spirit was wreaking havoc in hell. But the third day! On the third day he came breaking forth from the

chains of death, and from that time forth
Christians have referred to it as "The Lord's
Day", and have celebrated, on a weekly basis,
the conquering resurrection of Jesus from the
dead.

What The Resurrection Was *Not*

Some people think Lazarus was
resurrected. He was not. He was resuscitated.
When Jesus called Lazarus out of the tomb
(in John 11), Lazarus came walking back into
this life, he didn't come out of the grave with a
new kind of life that had conquered death.
Lazarus died twice! Once just before Jesus
resuscitated him, and again, later, when he
died a death just like all of us. Lazarus is dead
now. His body lies in some tomb somewhere in
Israel, now long forgotten.

C.S. Lewis wrote a wonderful poem, *Stephen to
Lazarus*, in which the martyr Stephen speaks
to Lazarus about his greater sacrifice:

> *But was I the first martyr, who*
> *Gave up no more than life, while you,*
> *Already free among the dead,*
> *Your rags stripped off, your fetters shed,*
> *Surrendered what all other men*
> *Irrevocably keep, and when*
> *Your battered ship at anchor lay*

Seemingly safe in the dark bay
No ripple stirs, obediently
Put out a second time to sea
Well knowing that your death (in vain
Died once) must all be died again?[3]

The resurrection of Jesus from the dead was not a resuscitation back to *this* life.

Neither was the resurrection a ghostly appearance, some kind of spiritual showing of a disembodied soul. People who think of the resurrection as a spiritual thing - akin to a seance or a ghost appearing - completely miss the point the Gospels make. When Jesus rose from the dead he had a *body* - a transformed and glorified body, but a body nonetheless. He ate fish sandwiches with the disciples on the lakeshore (John 21.4-14), Thomas touched his wounds (John 20.26-28) , and he broke bread with the two disciples on the road to Emmaus (Luke 24.13-35).

Finally, and this should go without saying, but some modern writers have actually suggested it, the resurrection was not a psychological imagining of his followers. Some people, claiming to be Christian yet unable to

---

[3] Lewis, C.S., *Poems*, New York, Harcourt Brace Jovanavich, 1964, p. 125.

accept the Christian belief in miracles, have said that what really happened was Jesus rose again *in the hearts* of his disciples, and that what we have here is a *resurrection of love*. You know, that's so silly I'm not even going to comment on it. Well, just one thing. In addition to seeing and writing about his bodily appearances, these 11 men went on to be persecuted and die for what they had seen and experienced. If it had been a resurrection of love in their hearts, they wouldn't have gone to the death for it.

What The Resurrection Was

The first thing I want to point out is that the resurrection was *unexpected*! This is a hugely significant point when considering the veracity of the matter. No one was expecting the Messiah to die and rise again. The Jews were looking for a strong and powerful military deliverer in their Messiah. When Jesus was crucified like a common criminal the disciples were dejected and went back to their boats and old lives. Jesus' resurrection wasn't even on the map of their minds. Even after it happened, they doubted (Luke 24.11, 38-41, Mark 16.11-14). Have you ever noticed this humorous passage: "Later Jesus appeared to the Eleven as they were eating; he rebuked them for their lack of faith and their stubborn refusal to believe those who had seen him after he had risen" (Mark 16.14)? Not only was the idea of a singular human resurrection foreign to Judaism, it was also foreign to the rest of religions. While other religions held the idea of the dying and rebirthing of a god, no other religion before Christianity claimed that a *man* had conquered death.

It is important to emphasize that what happened in the resurrection of Jesus was a passing *through* death and out the other side. Jesus didn't go down to death and then come back to a normal kind of life. He went down to death, conquered it and came out with a new, unique, supernatural (it had its source in God) and eternal kind of life. While his resurrection was physical - remember he ate with the disciples and they touched him (consider that beautiful passage from 1 John 1.1: "That which was from the beginning, which we have *heard*, which we have *seen* with our eyes, which we have *looked* at and our hands have *touched* — this we proclaim concerning the Word of life.") - it was also *transcendent*. Although he rose in a body, after the resurrection Jesus' body, while still the same, was also different. It had properties that were beyond the natural. He could walk through unopened doors. He could appear and disappear. It was as if (and it really was) that his body existed in two dimensions - the dimension of our world, and the dimension of the heavenly realm - and could pass in and out of our dimension at will.

The Effects Of The Resurrection

The resurrection of Jesus Christ was not an isolated incident that stands alone in the history of our salvation. Obviously it was closely related to his own death, but it also has implications that go far beyond that. First, in the resurrection, Christ himself was vindicated. When Peter and John performed a miracle of healing after the Day of Pentecost, they proclaimed, "Then know this, you and all the people of Israel: It is by the name of Jesus Christ of Nazareth, *whom you crucified but whom God raised from the dead*, that this man stands before you healed" (Acts 4.10). When Paul writes to Timothy and speaks of the resurrection, he uses the language that Christ "was *vindicated* by the Spirit" (1 Timothy 3.16). Jesus coming out of the grave was a vindication of all that he had taught, all that he had done, and all that he had claimed.

In his resurrection, Jesus vanquished death. Not only for himself, but for all who believe in him. Death lost its grip on Jesus (Acts 2.24), and it lost its power over man.

Paul wrote, "When the perishable has been clothed with the imperishable, and the mortal with immortality, then the saying that is written will come true: 'Death has been swallowed up in victory.' 'Where, O death, is your victory? Where, O death, is your sting?' The sting of death is sin, and the power of sin is the law. But thanks be to God! He gives us the victory through our Lord Jesus Christ" (1 Corinthians 15.54-47). In the resurrection of Christ, not only was *his* death vanquished, but so is *our* death - through his resurrection we have the hope of our own resurrection.

Not only did the resurrection of Jesus effect his own vindication and the vanquishing of death, but - and here is the main thing - in his resurrection *the New Creation was begun*! When Saint Paul wrote about this new creation, he became downright giddy! Next to the subject of salvation by grace this seems to be Paul's favorite theme: "We were therefore buried with him through baptism into death in order that, just as Christ was raised from the dead through the glory of the Father, *we too may live a new life*. If we have been united with him like this in his death, we will certainly also be united with him in his resurrection" (Romans 6.4-5).

This new creation - this new kind and quality of life - is not something we receive after we die. It is something we receive *now* in Christ. We have already begun to live in eternal life. Jesus told his disciples, "I tell you the truth, whoever hears my word and believes him who sent me *has* eternal life and will not be condemned; he *has* crossed over from death to life" (John 5.24). To the church in Corinth Paul wrote, "Therefore, if anyone is in Christ, he is a new creation; the old has gone, the new has come!" (2 Corinthians 5.17).

N.T. Wright, the bishop of Durham, England, and a prolific and trustworthy author, puts it like this: "When the Bible speaks of heaven and earth it is not talking about two localities related to each other within the same space-time continuum or about a nonphysical world contrasted with a physical one but about two different *kinds* of what we call space, two different kinds of what we call matter, and also quite possibly...two different kinds of what we call time...God's space and ours - heaven and earth, in other words - are, though very different, not far away from one another. Nor is talk about heaven simply a metaphorical way of talking about our own spiritual lives. God's space and ours interlock and intersect in a whole variety of ways even while they retain, for the moment at least, their separate and distinct identities and roles. One day...they will be joined in a quite new way, open and visible to one another, married together forever."[4]

The union of the two realms, to which we look forward and for which we live and pray and work, is already a reality in the resurrection of Jesus Christ.

Finally, the resurrection of Jesus was a securing of our own resurrection. In his *tour de force* chapter on the resurrection, Paul wrote, "If only for this life we have hope in Christ, we are to be pitied more than all men" (1 Corinthians 15.19). If we have no hope of the resurrection (and by this I do *not* mean "going to heaven"), then we have no hope at all. Paul tells us, rather, "But Christ has indeed been raised from the dead, the firstfruits of those who have fallen asleep. For since death came through a man, the resurrection of the dead comes also through a man. For as in Adam all die, so in Christ all will be made alive. But each in his own turn: Christ, the firstfruits; then, when he comes, those who belong to

---

[4] N.T. Wright, *Surprised by Hope*, New York, Harper, 2008, p. 114.

him. Then the end will come, when he hands over the kingdom to God the Father after he has destroyed all dominion, authority and power. For he must reign until he has put all his enemies under his feet. The last enemy to be destroyed is death" (1 Corinthians 15.20-26).

The resurrection of Jesus Christ is the most glorious truth of the Christian faith. It is the foundation of our hope. It establishes the grounds from which we stand and live (even as we *now* live in the power of the resurrection), and it shows the future we will experience and enjoy ourselves.

Chapter Seven

He Ascended Into Heaven

The Apostles' Creed:
"He ascended into heaven, and sits on the right hand of God the Father almighty."

The Nicene Creed:
"And ascended into heaven, and sits on the right hand of the Father."

Both Creeds skip over the whole of church history in the space of a sentence. They move from the ascension of Jesus to the second coming of Jesus, and these two events serve as "bookends" for church history. Church history proper began with the Day of Pentecost (Acts 2), when the Holy Spirit was poured out on 120 people who were praying together, and the New Testament Church was birthed. This occurred only a week and a half after the ascension of Christ into heaven, and was directly related to it. Church history proper will end with the second coming of the Lord. And so in this one line - "He ascended into heaven and...from there he shall come..." is found the entire flow of the story of the Church.

Exit Stage Left?

The ascension is the opposite of the incarnation. In the incarnation, God the Son *descended*, first to earth, and then to death, and even to hell. As we have already seen, in the lowest levels of hell "the great reversal" began. Christ rose from the dead, stayed with his disciples for forty days teaching them things concerning the Kingdom of God, and then took them up on a hill and *ascended* to heaven, surrounded by clouds.

I am convinced this is one of the most overlooked episodes in the life of Jesus. A lot of Christians give it no thought at all, and a lot of sermons kind of gloss over it making it nothing more than "exit, stage left" - the way that Jesus got off the stage and out of the picture - I mean, come on - he couldn't hang around here forever, right? This way of thinking completely misses the importance of the ascension. It wasn't "exit, stage left". It was the coronation of the King of the universe!

To grasp the ascension we must see it in the context of Old Testament prophecy. The ascension wasn't something that happened out of the blue and which no one expected. Daniel foresaw it. And how he described it is startling. But before we read the passage I must warn you: too many people have read this without care and have assumed it was a text about the second coming of Christ, what with all the clouds and fanfare and angels. Pay *close* attention: "In my vision at night I looked, and there before me was one like a son of man, coming with the clouds of heaven. He approached the Ancient of Days and was led into his presence. He was given authority, glory and sovereign power; all peoples, nations and men of every language worshiped him. His dominion is an everlasting dominion that will not pass away, and his kingdom is one that will never be destroyed" (Daniel 7.13-14).

Did you notice it? Look again at the text and ask yourself the question, "To *where* did the Son of Man come, all surrounded by the clouds of heaven?" Think about it.

Upon a second look it becomes clear that he came before the Ancient of Days (an

Old Testament title for God the Father). Now I ask you, when in the Bible does the Son of Man, surrounded by clouds, go to the Father? Luke records the scene: "So when they met together, they asked him, 'Lord, are you at this time going to restore the kingdom to Israel?' He said to them: 'It is not for you to know the times or dates the Father has set by his own authority. But you will receive power when the Holy Spirit comes on you; and you will be my witnesses in Jerusalem, and in all Judea and Samaria, and to the ends of the earth.' After he said this, *he was taken up before their very eyes, and a cloud hid him from their sight.* They were looking intently up into the sky as he was going, when suddenly two men dressed in white stood beside them. 'Men of Galilee,' they said, 'why do you stand here looking into the sky? This same Jesus, who has been taken from you into heaven, will come back in the same way you have seen him go into heaven'" (Acts 1.6-11).

What Daniel prophesied in chapter 7 was not the second coming of Christ, but his ascension. And please note what occurred at the ascension.

The Enthronement of Christ

Daniel said, "He was given authority, glory and sovereign power; all peoples, nations and men of every language worshiped him. His dominion is an everlasting dominion that will not pass away, and his kingdom is one that will never be destroyed". The ascension of Jesus was his coronation, his enthronement. Think about it - on that day a human being sat down on the throne of God! God, who became man, elevated his manhood into the heavenlies, not to sit *near* the throne, but to sit *on* the throne! When John got a glimpse of the heavenly throne room he saw this: "Then I saw a Lamb, looking as if it had been slain, standing in the center of the throne, encircled by the four living creatures and the elders" (Revelation 5.6). The Lamb of God - Christ - enthroned! Then John heard the angels and the twenty four elders singing, "You are worthy to take the scroll and to open its seals, because you were slain, and with your blood you purchased men for God from every tribe and language and people and nation. You have made them to be a kingdom and priests to serve our God, and they will reign on the earth" (Revelation 5.9-10). Notice the similarity to Daniel. Daniel saw the Son of Man being given authority and "all peoples, nations and men of every language worshiped him"; John saw the Lamb upon the throne after he had been slain and raised, and had "purchased men for God from every tribe and language and people and nation" and had "made them to be a kingdom and priests to serve our God".

Some modern popular Bible teachers tell us that Jesus will be made King when he comes back; that the Kingdom of God will begin at the second coming. The Bible teaches that the Kingdom of God began in the life, ministry, death and resurrection of Jesus, that the ceremony of his coronation was held at his ascension, and that he has brought us all - as priests who offer the sacrifice of praise - into his kingdom.

Let me pause to give you a little hint about reading the Gospels. When Matthew, Mark, Luke and John wrote, they often wrote in a sort of "shorthand". They would mention one phrase from the Old Testament, and their readers who were steeped in the Old Testament would automatically understand the entire context, the whole story. The same kind of thing happens with us in every day conversation. If someone says, "It was like 9/11," everyone in the modern world understands the "back story". No one retells the entire tale of the events that transpired in

110

New York City on September 11, 2001, but the simple saying of the numbers, "9/11" brings the whole story to mind. The same is true in the Gospels (and Epistles). When the writers use just a line from the Old Testament - "the abomination that causes desolation" or "the Son of Man coming on clouds of glory" - unlike most modern readers, the knowledgeable original readers understood everything *behind* those phrases.

In the second Gospel Saint Mark tells us a bit more about the ascension: "After the Lord Jesus had spoken with them, he was taken up into heaven and *he sat at the right hand of God*" (Mark 16.19). When Mark wrote this he wasn't just making up words. He was referencing another famous Old Testament coronation passage - the most quoted Psalm in the New Testament, Psalm 2, and it bears being read in full (but note especially the italicized words):

> 1 Why do the nations conspire
>   and the peoples plot in vain?
>
> 2 The kings of the earth take their stand
>   and the rulers gather together
>   against the Lord
>   and against his Anointed One.

3 "Let us break their chains," they say,
  "and throw off their fetters."

4 The One enthroned in heaven laughs;
  the Lord scoffs at them.

5 Then he rebukes them in his anger
  and terrifies them in his wrath,
  saying,

6 *"I have installed my King
  on Zion, my holy hill."*

7 I will proclaim the decree of the
  Lord :
    He said to me, *"You are my Son;
    today I have become your Father.*

8 *Ask of me, and I will make the nations
  your inheritance,
    the ends of the earth your possession.*

9 You will rule them with an iron
  scepter;
    you will dash them to pieces like
    pottery."

10 Therefore, you kings, be wise;
   be warned, you rulers of the earth.

11 Serve the Lord with fear

and rejoice with trembling.

12 Kiss the Son, lest he be angry
    and you be destroyed in your way,
    for his wrath can flare up in a
    moment.
    Blessed are all who take refuge in
    him.

When Christ was enthroned, when he
was crowned as King after having victoriously
defeated all his enemies, leading the powers of
hell in a parade of victory and making them a
public spectacle (Colossians 2.15), he asked
the Father, and the nations were made his (cf.
Acts 13.33, Hebrews 1.5), and he "sat down at
the Father's right hand" - this is one more bit
of "shorthand", quoted from Psalm 2. To sit is
the position of ruling (enthronement) and the
right hand of the Father is not a literal *place* (as
if God the Father had a right hand), but a
picture of power and authority - to sit at a
King's right hand meant to be second only to
him in rank. When the Bible uses this
language of Jesus in relation to the Father it is
not speaking literally or spatially - it is saying
that the Man Christ Jesus is second only to
the Father (cf. 1 Corinthians 15.27-28).
Christ is on his throne. The Kingdom of God
is not something we are waiting for, it is
something we are *living in*!

Our Great High Priest

There is one more mention of Psalm 2 that deserves our attention in relation to the ascension. Not only was Jesus crowned as King in the ascension, he was also firmly established as our High Priest. He did the work of a high priest in his sacrifice on the cross (being both the priest and the sacrifice - "sacrificing himself"), but when he ascended, he entered into a heavenly Holy of Holies there to function as a high priest on our behalf.

In Hebrews 5 we read, "Every high priest is selected from among men and is appointed to represent them in matters related to God, to offer gifts and sacrifices for sins. He is able to deal gently with those who are ignorant and are going astray, since he himself is subject to weakness. This is why he has to offer sacrifices for his own sins, as well as for the sins of the people. No one takes this honor upon himself; he must be called by God, just as Aaron was. So Christ also did not take upon himself the glory of becoming a high priest. But God said to him, *'You are my Son; today I have become your Father.'* And he says in another place, 'You are a priest forever, in the order of Melchizedek.' During the days of

Jesus' life on earth, he offered up prayers and petitions with loud cries and tears to the one who could save him from death, and he was heard because of his reverent submission. Although he was a son, he learned obedience from what he suffered and, once made perfect, he became the source of eternal salvation for all who obey him and was designated by God to be high priest in the order of Melchizedek" (Hebrews 5.1-10).

Later, Hebrews tells us, "Now there have been many of those priests, since death prevented them from continuing in office; but *because Jesus lives forever*, he has a *permanent priesthood*. Therefore he is able to save completely those who come to God through him, because he always lives to intercede for them" (Hebrews 7.23-25).

Do you understand what Hebrews is telling us so far? That Christ is our High Priest, and that unlike other high priests, he lives forever, therefore his ministry is ongoing. Now the writer tells us that the ministry of Christ, unlike other high priests, takes place in heaven. Note carefully the language:

"The point of what we are saying is this: We do have such a high priest, *who sat down at the right hand of the throne of the Majesty in heaven,* and who serves in the sanctuary, the true tabernacle set up by the Lord, not by man. Every high priest is appointed to offer both gifts and sacrifices, and so it was necessary for this one also to have something to offer. If he were on earth, he would not be a priest, for there are already men who offer the gifts prescribed by the law. They serve at a sanctuary that is a copy and shadow of what is in heaven" (Hebrews 8.1-5).

"For Christ did not enter a man-made sanctuary that was only a copy of the true one; *he entered heaven itself,* now to appear for us in God's presence. Nor did he enter heaven to offer himself again and again, the way the high priest enters the Most Holy Place every year with blood that is not his own. Then Christ would have had to suffer many times since the creation of the world. But now he has appeared *once for all* at the end of the ages to *do away with sin* by the sacrifice of himself. Just as man is destined to die once, and after that to face judgment, so Christ was sacrificed once to take away the sins of many people; and he will appear a second time, not to bear sin, but to bring salvation to those who are waiting for him" (Hebrews 9.24-27).

I know that's a *lot* of information from Hebrews! But I hope you see the point: Christ is the sacrifice - he died on the cross once for all and took away the sins of the whole world! But that is not all. He rose again, and ascended into heaven, and was enthroned and from there continues his ministry as our great High Priest. In the "eternal now" of the heavenly realm, the sacrifice offered by Christ continues to do its work, and when he comes again it will be without regard to sin (for that has already been dealt with - "done away with"), but to complete our salvation - the resurrection from the dead and the new creation of heaven and earth!

Sender of the Holy Spirit

As if the ascension wasn't significant enough in regard to his kingship and priesthood, it also marks the mechanism for the sending of the Holy Spirit to the Church and the birth of the New Covenant people.

Jesus told his disciples that he was going away, and he was a bit disappointed that none of them asked him, 'Where?" - because of their grief (John 16.5-6). They didn't get it! His going away was not a final departure, but to accomplish a great work. They shouldn't be filled with grief; if they only knew "where" he was going they would be jumping for joy! He was going to his enthronement. He was going to his priestly temple. He was going to the Father. And he was going to continue his work by sending the Holy Spirit: "I tell you the truth: It is for your good that I am going away. Unless I go away, the Counselor will not come to you; but if I go, I will send him to you" (John 16.7).

In Acts, standing there on the side of the mountain, having spent forty days after his resurrection teaching the disciples about the Kingdom of God, the final thing Jesus told them was, "Do not leave Jerusalem, but wait for the gift my Father promised, which you have heard me speak about. For John baptized with water, but in a few days you will be baptized with the Holy Spirit...you will receive power when the Holy Spirit comes on you; and you will be my witnesses in Jerusalem, and in all Judea and Samaria, and to the ends of the earth" (Acts 1.4-8). And then he ascended - not as the final act of his ministry among us, but as the first great act of worldwide evangelization and victory! The ascension of Christ into the heavenly realm isn't his getaway after all! It is the moment of his enthronement as King, and his entering the heavenly sanctuary as High Priest and his empowerment of his people to do the work he called them to do.

Chapter Eight

He Shall Come Again

Apostles' Creed:
"From there he shall come to judge the living and the dead."

Nicene Creed:
"And he shall come again, with glory, to judge both the living and the dead; whose kingdom shall have no end."

   Bookends. The ascension of Christ and his second coming are bookends to the Church age. The era of the Church (the era we live in now) began with Christ ascending to heaven and pouring out the Holy Spirit ten days later, and church history as we know it will come to an end when he comes again to bring to fulfillment the new creation which has already begun in his resurrection.

The Creeds do not address the details leading up to the coming of the Lord, and Christians have argued over these matters for centuries. One of the most extreme (and newest, by the way) ideas happens to be a very popular one currently. It divides history up into seven different eras, seven "dispensations" in the plan of God, each of which finds God relating to people differently. We are told that we are living in the next to the last era - the Age of Grace - and that it will end with cataclysmic events including a secret rapture of believers from off the planet, the emergence of an evil figure called the Antichrist, and a horrible period of time on earth called the Great Tribulation. I have argued elsewhere that this novel idea has no true place in the teaching of the Church and is actually a misreading of Scripture.[5]

But my point now is that this is not the point. Whatever your views about what comes before the second coming, what the Creeds affirm is that there *will be* a second coming. Jesus, who ascended into heaven, will come

---

[5] See *The End Is Near...Or Maybe Not*, audio series by Kenneth Myers; Sherman, TX; Graceworks; 2008.

again, "in the same way you have seen him go into heaven", or as the King James Version so majestically gives it, "This same Jesus, which is taken up from you into heaven, shall so come in like manner as ye have seen him go into heaven" (Acts 1.11).

A Word About The Word *Coming*

When the New Testament writers (the Apostles themselves) speak of the second coming of Christ they use an important word that has a special nuance. Unfortunately, it doesn't come across in other languages with that same nuance. The word is *parousia*, and it literally means "to be present" or "to become present". An English word that is a better translation (but which has mostly fallen out of use in common speech) is *advent*. We may say something like, "With the advent of the automobile the use of horse and buggy fell away." What we mean by that is when automobiles "became present" not many people stuck to horses as their means of transportation. We aren't talking about the *event* of the automobile showing up on the scene, but the *presence* of automobiles in the world.

The New International Version actually translates *parousia* as "presence" when Paul speaks about his own body: "For his letters, say they, are weighty and powerful; but his bodily *presence* is weak, and his speech contemptible. Let such an one think this, that, such as we are in word by letters when we are absent, such will we be also in deed when we are *present*" (2 Corinthians 10.10-11).

There are other words the New Testament writers could have used if their primary focus was on the act of coming (traveling from one place and going to another), but they chose to use this carefully nuanced word because their point was the arrival and presence of Jesus. In light of this definition, reconsider some verses from the Bible:

> •"For as in Adam all die, even so in Christ shall all be made alive. But every man in his own order: Christ the firstfruits; afterward they that are Christ's at his *coming*" (1 Corinthians 15.22-23).
> •"For what is our hope, our joy, or the crown in which we will glory in the presence of our Lord Jesus when he *comes*?" (1 Thessalonians 2.19).

•"May he strengthen your hearts so
that you will be blameless and holy in
the presence of our God and Father
when our Lord Jesus *comes* with all his
holy ones" (1 Thessalonians 3.13).
•"Be patient, then, brothers, until the
Lord's *coming*" (James 5.7).

In this sampling (there are many more
similar verses), all of them are best read as as
referring to "the advent" or "the arrival and
presence" or "the being here" of the Lord.

Heaven Isn't A Place

The reason the carefully nuanced word
is so important is that it points to a reality we
creatures of three dimensions often miss. We
think of heaven as a *place*. It is "out there".
Where? Well, maybe beyond the galaxies,
maybe beyond the limits of the universe. But
we still think of it as a place that is in relation
to all other places. When we think of the
ascension it is almost unavoidable for us to
think of Jesus going from *here* (a place) to *there*
(another place).

But for lack of a better word, we should
think of heaven, not as another place in the
same time/space dimension as our world, but

as another *dimension*, another way of existence. Heaven is the very presence of God, and God is omnipresent. Heaven isn't "there". Heaven is here, there, and everywhere. Jesus "came down from heaven" in the incarnation. He stepped out of the heavenly dimension and into our three-dimensional world. When he rose from the dead in a physical body and ascended into heaven, he took a physical body - a body from *our* dimension - *into* the heavenly dimension!

After his resurrection, and before his ascension, Jesus seemed to appear from nowhere and then disappear back into nowhere. Think of it in light of the heavenly dimension. Jesus having in himself joined Deity and Humanity together, is a single person with two natures - one nature of the earth, one nature of the heavenly realm. Therefore, after the resurrection, we see him moving easily back and forth between the two realms. *In him the two realms are joined together.* In him, as the hymn says, "earth and heaven are one."

Even after his ascension we find him "showing up". Saul of Tarsus has an encounter with him on the road to Damascus. Throughout history we hear of various godly people "seeing" Jesus. He is not some *place* else 50 billion miles away. He is in heaven, and heaven, if we can accept it, is at our fingertips ("the kingdom of heaven is *at hand*," Jesus said - Matthew 4.17, KJV). But what has all this to do with the second coming? I'm glad you asked.

He Shall Be Present

Jesus is coming back. On the last day (and not a day before, I would argue) he is returning. And when I say Jesus is coming back, I don't mean he is coming from one place in the world (far, far away) to our place in the world. I mean that he is going to bring the two dimensions together! He is going to appear in our realm because he is laying hold of our realm and dragging it into the heavenlies, joining the two together forever, and suddenly we will all find ourselves - body, soul and spirit - resurrected and living fully in the new creation! Christ isn't coming back to take us all away. He is coming back to finish what he started, to bring to fulfillment the purpose of the Father, to fully reconcile this created dimension with that uncreated dimension.

Too many Christians think the end goal of life is to "die and go to heaven", but this is nowhere the message of the New Testament.

The message of the Apostles is that Jesus has risen from the dead and has initiated the new creation, that we are all citizens of that realm, and that we look forward to the day of his return - his advent, his arrival, his presence - when we too shall put on immortality and be made like him.

When Paul writes of that "blessed hope" he tells us, "But Christ has indeed been raised from the dead, the firstfruits of those who have fallen asleep...so in Christ all will be made alive. But each in his own turn: Christ, the firstfruits; then, when he *comes [parousia - when he is made present]*, those who belong to him...then the Son himself will be made subject to him who put everything under him, so that God may be all in all" (1 Corinthians 15.20-28).

John tells us, "Dear friends, now we are children of God, and what we will be has not yet been made known. But we know that when he appears, *we shall be like him*, for we shall see him as he is" (1 John 3.2).

It is not only us - Christians, humans - who will be "changed", but the Bible teaches us that all nature will be changed. Some people have an idea of the future that goes something like this: Jesus is going to come back from a place far, far away, and he is going to take us away with him, back to that place, and the earth is going to be blown to smithereens! Unfortunately, this misunderstanding has even made it into a common phrase of the English language: "blown to kingdom come". This is a far cry from what the Bible actually teaches about creation itself. Paul tells us that creation is "standing on tiptoe" (to use a phrase from *The New Testament in Modern English*) looking forward to *our* resurrection, because when that happens, creation itself will *also* be made new and set free from its own fallen nature: "I consider that our present sufferings are not worth comparing with the glory that will be revealed in us. The creation waits in eager expectation for the sons of God to be revealed. For the creation was subjected to frustration, not by its own choice, but by the will of the one who subjected it, in hope that the *creation itself will be liberated from its bondage to decay* and brought into the glorious freedom of the children of God. We know that the whole creation has been groaning as in the pains of childbirth right up to the present time. Not only so, but we ourselves, who have the firstfruits of the Spirit, groan inwardly as we wait eagerly for our adoption as sons, *the redemption of our bodies*. For in this hope we were saved" (Romans 8.18-24).

Jesus is coming back. And when he does, he is bringing heaven with him.

To Judge the Living and the Dead

Some Christians, because they do not understand the great work of reconciliation and forgiveness of sins that Jesus accomplished on the cross, live in terror of God and in terror of the second coming. Their sentiment is captured in a bumper-sticker that can be seen now and then, "Jesus is coming back...and boy is he mad!".

Both creeds say Jesus is coming to "judge the living and the dead". We need to understand what Jesus himself had to say about judgment. In the Gospel of John, chapter five, we find Jesus' discourse regarding everlasting life, resurrection from the dead, and judgment. Several important elements should be noted.

First, the Father has given the job of judging to the Son: "For just as the Father raises the dead and gives them life, even so the Son gives life to whom he is pleased to give it. Moreover, the Father judges no one, but has *entrusted all judgment* to the Son" (John 5.21-22).

Next, he goes into this amazing teaching regarding the eternal life which those who believe in him *already* possess (pay attention to the italics, they are important): "I tell you the truth, whoever hears my word and believes him who sent me *has* eternal life and *will not be condemned*; he *has crossed over from death to life*. I tell you the truth, a time is coming and *has now come* when the dead will hear the voice of the Son of God and those who hear will live" (John 5.24-25). If you believe in Jesus, you already have eternal life, you are already free from condemnation (now and on the last day) and you have already experienced a resurrection - you have already crossed over from death to life.

Finally, he speaks of the last day when *everyone* will rise from the grave: "Do not be amazed at this, for a time *is coming* when *all* who are in their graves will hear his voice and come out—those who have done good will rise to live, and those who have done evil will rise to be condemned" (John 5.28-29). There is a condemnation on the last day, but it is not for believers. No one accidentally finds themselves condemned. Who, then, stands condemned on the last day?

This next bit needs your careful attention. We have already seen that the Father doesn't judge, but leaves that job to the Son. Now watch what Jesus says about his own judging: "You judge by human standards; *I pass judgment on no one*" (John 8.15). Jesus clearly states that he judges *no one*!

And now, here is the *pièce de résistance*: "As for the person who hears my words but does not keep them, *I do not judge him*. For I did not come to judge the world, but to save it. *There is a judge* for the one who rejects me and does not accept my words; *that very word which I spoke* will condemn him at the last day (John 12.47-48). Jesus has made it clear - more than once - that he is not in the judging business. He is not out to condemn anyone. He is out to save anyone and everyone who will accept his salvation. And if you do accept it - if you do believe in him - you will not be condemned. Paul would later write, "Therefore, there is now *no condemnation* for those who are in Christ Jesus" (Romans 8.1).

What judges people on the last day is their rejection of Jesus' word. And the word he brings is the "good news" that in his life, death and resurrection he has reconciled the world to himself; the only thing required is a life that says, "Yes!" to his already accomplished reconciliation. The point is, no one accidentally gets condemned on the last day. People are condemned for the perpetual refusal to accept the mercy of God. The Father judges no one. The Son judges no one. People judge themselves. God sends no one to hell. They go there of their own accord ("Hell's doors are locked from the inside," says C.S. Lewis).

There is one final dimension to judgment that should be noted. The Greek word is *krisis* (from which we get our English word crisis) and it means to decide between the two. Most people hear the word "judgment" and automatically think of punishment, but that is not at all the idea. The real work of a judge is to *make things right*. To establish justice and equity. Yes, on the last day there will be reward, and there will be condemnation for those who refuse the free gift of eternal life. But what really happens on the last day - the "meta-story" as they say, is that God will make everything right! What was lost in Adam and what has begun to be restored in the resurrection of Jesus and the Holy Spirit's presence in the Church will be fully and finally restored. In the words of Lady Julian of Norwich, "And all shall be well. And all shall be well. And all manner of things shall be well."

Chapter Nine

I Believe In The Holy Spirit

Apostles' Creed:
"I believe in the Holy Spirit."

Nicene Creed:
"And I believe in the Holy Spirit, the Lord
and giver of life, who proceeds from the
Father and the Son; who with the Father and
the Son together is worshipped and glorified;
who spoke by the Prophets."

"I believe in the Holy Spirit." With this
line we come to the third and final clause of
the creeds. The first clause spoke of God the
Father. The second clause of God the Son.
Now we turn to God the Holy Spirit.

The Lord and Giver of Life

God the Father, the Son, and the Holy
Spirit - and yet, as Saint Athanasius wrote,
"there be not three Gods, but one God". The
fact that the creeds focus on God as Father,
Son and Holy Spirit in no way suggests God is
three different beings. Christians are not
tritheists. Whatever else can be said about the
Christian faith, it agrees with the great *Schema*
of Deuteronomy 6.4, "Hear O Israel, the
Lord, the Lord is *one*."

In studying the first clause of the Creed
we saw that God the Father is that invisible,
untouchable, unapproachable "inner" aspect of
God - God in himself. In studying the second
clause we learned that God the Son, far from
coming into existence in the incarnation, is
"eternally begotten" of the Father, that is, he is
always in the process of being "published",
being "sent forth", and is indeed the only
manifestation of the invisible God (Hebrews
1.3 says that the Son is "the exact
representation of his being" and Paul writes in
Colossians 1.15 that "He is the image of the
invisible God"). If the Father is the Generator,
and the Son is the Generated, then the Holy
Spirit is the Generation. He is the life, the
breath (Hebrew: *ruach*; Greek: *pneuma*), the
power, and the energy of God.

But the Spirit is not simply something related to God or coming from him. The Creed is careful to make this distinction by calling him Lord. The same things that we learned about the term Lord being applied to Christ (see Chapter Three) also apply here. The Holy Spirit *is* the One True God. The Holy Spirit is Yahweh. He is of the same singular substance as the Father and the Son.

The Holy Spirit, as God himself, is, the Nicene Creed declares, "the giver of life". He is the God who in the beginning hovered over the face of the deep and brought creation into form. He is the same God who was breathed into the dust-made body of Adam and made him a living soul. He is the same God "in whom we live and move and have our being" to quote Paul (in Acts 17.28; he was quoting the Greek Poet Epimenides, who had said the same thing 600 years before him).

Who Proceeds from the Father...uh...and the Son

I hate church fights. I've been a member of the clergy since I was 20 years old (that's 30 years now), and I have *never* enjoyed church fights. I have been in a few, but I never liked them. But I have never been in church fights like the ones that happened around the year 1000 in Europe and Asia. In 1054 the Church split right down the middle. You think a little congregation splitting over which version of the Bible to use is chaotic. What I'm talking about was the mother of all church splits. It is remembered to this day as "The Great Schism" and it is a sad and tragic chapter in our family story.

Since this is not a book on church history I won't go into great details, but I will say that part of what caused that terrible division in the Body of Christ was the little phrase, "and the Son" (in Latin, *filioque*). It's called the *filioque* clause, and it became symbolic of all that was divisive between the Eastern Church (now called the Orthodox Churches) and the Western Church (now called the Roman Catholic Church, along with all its later splinters of Protestantism).

The short version goes like this. When the Nicene Creed was originally written (A.D. 325 and 381) it was considered an *ecumenical statement*. That means that the *whole* Church agreed to it, got behind it, and published it. It wasn't to be monkeyed with, except by a council of the *whole* Church. But in Toledo, Spain, in 589, the Christians were fighting a fresh batch of Arian heresy and to strengthen the understanding that Jesus was God they added that the Holy Spirit proceeded not only from the Father, but "from the Son". They meant well, but after a while the Eastern Church started saying that the Western Church had no authority to change the Creed unilaterally. They never declared the clause heretical, they just said that only the whole Church had the authority to modify the Creed. The Western Church defended what had been done, claimed that it *did too* have the authority because it had the Pope, and ended up adopting the clause throughout all Europe. Centuries later, when the Protestants broke away from the Roman Catholic Church they retained the Creed as they had always known it.

Granting that the Eastern Church has a point about not changing the Creed unilaterally, the theological question remains as to who was right and who was wrong? To answer that we have to learn two big words. I promise it won't hurt. Much. The words are *ontological* and *epistemological*.

Ontology has to do with the study of the nature of a thing, the being of a thing (from the Greek *ontos*, meaning *being*). A caterpillar may change into a butterfly, but it is *ontologically* still the same creature. If we approach this creedal question from an ontological argument, the East is right. The Holy Spirit, who is the life and energy of God proceeds from Father, who is the invisible "inner" God, and the result is the manifestation of the Son, who is the revealed God. Ontologically speaking, the Spirit does not proceed from the Father and the Son, but proceeds from the Father alone (a very weak analogy is to think of the sun: the sun itself [the Father] generates a beam of light [the Spirit] but what is *seen*, what is *revealed* is the light hitting our eyes [the Son]. OK, enough for weak analogies). Score one for the Orthodox.

Epistemology is the study of a thing as it is known, as a thing is understood from outside itself (from the Greek *episteme*, meaning knowledge). From an epistemological argument the West is right. The way we understand the Holy Spirit coming to *us* is that he comes from the Father and the Son. After all, Jesus said, "It is for your good that I am going away. Unless I go away, the Counselor will not come to you; but if I go, *I* will send him to you" (John 16.7). Jesus, God the Son, went to the Father, and the Spirit of God was sent to us. Score one for the Western Church.

But this phrase (and other important disagreements, like the universal authority of the Bishop of Rome) caused both sides to get very testy with one another, excommunicate one another, and endure a millennium of bitterness, rivalry and competition. Score a big fat zero for both sides. Thankfully, in our own time, the Christian families of East and West are trying to work things out and smooth things over and come into unity and get on with what Jesus called them to do: love one another and spread the Gospel throughout the whole world. Give both sides points for this.

Whew, I'm glad *that's* over with, and I bet you are too! But now back to the Creed itself: whichever version you opt for, it's correct.

Worshipped and Glorified

The Nicene Creed continues, "Who with the Father and the Son together is worshipped and glorified..." Here again is a statement of the divinity of the Spirit. The Spirit is not just the energy flowing from God, the Spirit *is* God. Only God is worshipped, and the Holy Spirit is worshipped. And here also is a declaration of the unity of God. God is One. We don't worship three different beings. We don't pray to the Father, and then pray to a different God in the Son, and then pray a third prayer to an additional third God in the Spirit. The phrase is, "with the Father and the Son together". We worship Father, Son and Holy Spirit - together - One God.

He Spoke by the Prophets

In the second century there was a nutcase named Marcion running around saying that the Old Testament era was the Age of the Father, that the New Testament era was the Age of the Son, and that *his* era was the Age of the Spirit. He published his own version of Scripture, leaving out the whole Old Testament, three of the Gospels, and including ten of Paul's letters after he edited out of them of any Old Testament references. He declared that he was the only one capable of truly understanding the faith, and saw the God of the Old Testament as a different "god" than Jesus, who was different from the Holy Spirit.

When the Creed says that the Holy Spirit "spoke by the prophets" it is saying that the Holy Spirit is not simply a New Testament development in our understanding of God. The Spirit *is* God, and therefore was at work from the beginning (Genesis 1.2) and before. It was he who inspired and directed and spoke through the prophets, pointing and preparing the way for the Messiah - for God to become flesh among us, and therefore the Old Testament prophets were not of a different god or a different religion than the Apostles.

The last prophet of the Old Covenant, John the Baptist, leapt in his mother's womb when Elizabeth was "filled with the Spirit" upon the visitation of the pregnant Virgin Mary (Luke 1.41-45), and at the occasion of that very John the Baptist baptizing Jesus in the Jordan river he saw the Holy Spirit descend on him in the form of a dove (Luke 3.21). The prophets of the Old Covenant were not in discontinuity with the New, they were forerunners of it, and rejoiced to see its day. And they were all moved along by the same Holy Spirit that we worship and glorify, that is, God himself.

Chapter Ten

One, Holy, Catholic and Apostolic Church

Apostles' Creed:
"The holy catholic Church, the communion of saints."

Nicene Creed:
"And I believe one, holy, catholic and apostolic Church."

There are something like twenty five thousand different denominations in the world today. Some of the older ones (and, oddly, newer ones too) claim that they are the only *real* church and that everyone else is at best playing games and at worst going straight to hell.

We learned in the previous chapter about The Great Schism of 1054, that first terrible tearing of the fabric of the Church. Since then, particularly in the West, that fragmentation has continued until we end up with what we have today - any given small town has within it at least a dozen different Christian church denominations. But before 1054 things were different. Up until that time there weren't different denominations, there was just "the Church". Some naive lovers of early church history like to imagine the first one thousand years as a kind of heaven on earth, Nirvana, Utopia, when everyone was loving and nice and united and godly. Of course this wasn't the case. Current church fights pale in comparison to the battles and intrigues of the first thousand years. But, in spite of all the rivalries, foolishness, deceit, ungodliness, and downright meanness, the one stellar thing that can be said about the early Church that cannot be said fully about the Church today is that it was one.

The older Apostles' Creed declares the Church to be holy and catholic. The later Nicene Creed adds two more markers - she is also one and apostolic.

One

When Jesus prayed for the Church he said, "My prayer is not for them alone. I pray also for those who will believe in me through their message, that all of them may *be one*, Father, just as you are in me and I am in you. May they also be in us so that the world may believe that you have sent me. I have given them the glory that you gave me, that they may be one as we are one: I in them and you in me. May they be brought to *complete unity* to let the world know that you sent me and have loved them even as you have loved me" (John 17.20-23).

If we give careful attention to Jesus' words, we find that he knew that the Church did not possess complete unity. He prayed to the Father that the Church would be "*brought to* complete unity." There was a process to be gone through. Later, when Paul wrote the Christians in Ephesus, he too recognized that complete unity had not been achieved in the Church. He told them that leadership had been established in the Church, "so that the body of Christ may be built up *until* we all reach unity in the faith and in the knowledge of the Son of God and become mature, attaining to the whole measure of the fullness of Christ" (Ephesians 4.12-13).

So no one should think that even in the golden apostolic years the church was ever completely at peace and unity within itself. Having said that, the first mark of defining the Church is unity. Although it has fragmented into many streams, God's desire is to see those streams reassemble into a great and mighty river that will fill the world. Christians ought to be committed to spiritually growing together with other Christians of different denominations, iron sharpening iron, until we achieve those very things which Jesus and Paul spoke of.

Even though the Church has been officially divided since 1054, and officially further splintered for the last five hundred years, in a deep spiritual sense, the Church *is* one. Yes there are Eastern Orthodox, Roman Catholics, Anglicans, Lutherans, Presbyterians, Baptists, Methodists, Congregationalists, Pentecostals, Charismatics, Non-denominationalists (which are just little denominations within themselves), independents and a host of other labels. And yes, these are all varyingly different in their practice and ethics and doctrines and disciplines. Yet there is still an underlying unity seen in two particular things.

First, true Christians of all stripes and colors possess faith in the person and works of Jesus Christ - that he is God come in the flesh to redeem mankind and that salvation is found in him. These believers are *in Christ*, and therefore, whether they know it or not, are at the deepest and most fundamental level at unity with one another.

Secondly, these believers all agree on basic Christian doctrine. They may fight with one another over minutiae, but regarding the essentials of the faith, they are close to one another. C.S. Lewis, the great English scholar and author, was an atheist who experienced a marvelous conversion to Christ. Later, as a Christian apologist, he described how amazingly united Christians seemed when viewed from the outside. They all possessed a common core faith. He went on to write a wonderful book on the subject titled *Mere Christianity*. If they could just recognize it, Christians have more that unites them than divides them.

Even so, the divisions that exist in the Church are not pleasing to God, and part of the work that Christians should be committed

to is the long and hard work of transcending
the barriers that divide us. This work is made
easier by the moving of the Holy Spirit who in
our own generation has done so much to tear
down the walls between believing brothers
and sisters. Five hundred years ago Roman
Catholics and Protestants were killing one
another. Now they pray and sing and even
speak in tongues together! Go figure. God is
at work.

Holy

Holiness has been given a bad name in
modern times. It has been misdefined as
legalism. Let me make it clear here and now:
holiness has *nothing to do* with legalism. People
have assumed that holiness means not playing
certain games, not drinking certain drinks, not
wearing certain fashions and hairstyles.
Nothing could be further from the truth.

When the Bible and the Church speak
of being holy, the idea is being *separate*. The
very word (both in Hebrew, *kadash*, and
Greek, *hagios*) means "to be set aside for a
special purpose". No one drinks root beer
from a sacred chalice. The chalice is set aside
for a special use - for celebrating the Lord's
Supper. Root beer is drunk from an ordinary
glass or even a paper cup. The chalice is holy.

This is not a moral statement in any way. The chalice isn't holy because it observes some legalistic set of rules; it is holy because it is set aside for special use. No bride-to-be would wear her wedding dress to go have breakfast at Denny's. First of all, everyone would look at her and think she was crazy. Secondly, she would spill gravy on it. But more importantly, the wedding dress is set aside for a special purpose - her wedding. That dress is not like other dresses. It is holy.

When God established his own New Covenant people, those people were called his "Church". The Greek term for church (*ekklesia*) is not a religious word at all, but a political one. It has to do with citizenship. It was used for a group of citizens being called out for a special meeting or task. When the New Testament writers use this word they are saying that God's people are a "called out people". God has called us out of the world (the powers that stand in opposition to him) and has called us to stand *over against* the world. The Church is to be defined by its *differentness* from the world. We are to live by God's standards, not fallen man's. We are to hold to God's values, not the values of our particular culture and age.

Saint Paul wrote to the Ephesians, "Consequently, you are no longer foreigners and aliens, but *fellow citizens* with God's people and members of God's household, built on the foundation of the apostles and prophets, with Christ Jesus himself as the chief cornerstone. In him the whole building is joined together and rises to become a *holy* temple in the Lord" (Ephesians 2.19-21). Holiness, then, is best understood as being faithful to God's revealed will as found in Scripture. Much of modern religion has sought to make Scripture palatable to the society of the day. In doing so there has been a dilution of God's will and an accommodation to sub-biblical norms. The mistake has been this: rather than a fresh application of God's word to society, there has been a reinterpretation of God's Word catering to society. As the Church, we are not to reinterpret Scripture according to our cultural norms. Rather, we are to bring the fresh application of God's Word to bear upon every aspect of life. This is what it means to be holy.

Catholic

Some of you hiccuped when you saw this word. Some of you jumped ahead to this page to see what I would say about it. To both groups I would propose that you have misunderstood the word. If the word holiness is much ill defined in our day, the word catholic is almost completely misunderstood. Actually the definition of catholic has nothing whatsoever to do with rosaries, Rome or the Pope. The *Roman* Catholic Church is simply one expression of the Catholic Church. More about that momentarily.

Catholic, defined perhaps oversimplistically, means *universal*. Not just universal in territory - "everywhere" - but universal in time as well. It means that the Church is for everyone in every place in every time.

Now for a less simple explanation. The word catholic comes from the Greek phrase *kath' holou* which means "of the whole". Everyone has heard of DNA and understands it at least a little bit. DNA is the "code" of our whole body which can be found in any particular part of our body. Scientists can take a cell from my nose or finger or knee - from my blood or skin or bone - and it will contain the DNA code for my whole body - it will tell what color my skin, hair and eyes are; it will tell my weight tendencies, whether I am male or female, what diseases I may be prone to. Amazing stuff, DNA. DNA strands are *catholic*. They are "of the whole". Each particular includes the whole, just as the whole is made up of all the particulars. Heady stuff!

In the same way, the word catholic implies that the fullness of the Church can be found in any "cell" of the Church (a cell being the nucleus of a bishop, surrounded by those who accompany him in the faith). The first person to apply the word to the Church was not some medieval Roman potentate, but a humble and godly martyr from the first century by the name of Ignatius. He was the bishop of Antioch (and was trained and ordained by the Apostles themselves) who found himself under arrest for being a Christian. On his way to being fed to the lions in Rome he wrote a letter to the church in Smyrna and said, "Wherever the bishop appears, the whole congregation is to be present, just as wherever Jesus Christ is, there is the *catholic* church" (Smyrneans 8.2).

When we say the Church is Catholic there are several implications. First, it means the Church is *inclusive*. It cannot be catholic and reject people because of race, sex or nationality. When a church refuses someone on the basis of skin color, social status or cultural difference, it loses its catholicity.

Second, it means the church is   *dependent*.
The Church's expression in a local
congregation is not independent. An
independent church should be an oxymoron.
It should be a contradiction of terms. If the
Church is catholic it is not locally
independent, but is simply a local expression
of the worldwide Church. There is, therefore,
a responsibility to interact with and heed the
rest of the Church.

Finally, it means the Church is
nonsectarian. The Church is not distinguished
by a unique doctrine, philosophy or practice.
The fact that we all have labels is a sad
commentary on the state of the Church today.
Ideally we should not be identified by whether
we are Charismatic or Pentecostal or Baptist
or Anglican or Roman or Orthodox or any of
the other distinctives that identify us. And
even if we are identified as such, that certainly
should not be the spirit in which we present
ourselves. There should never be an us/them
attitude in the Church. We are one, we are
called out, and we are "of the whole".

Apostolic

Apostolic, simply put, means coming
from the Apostles. The New Testament refers
frequently to the traditions received from the

Apostles, and the New Testament itself is simply the collected inspired written traditions of these followers of Jesus. Consider these verses. In each of them there is the idea of the *transmission* of apostolic *tradition* (the words *received* and *passed on* are technical terms for the "transmission of tradition"):

- "For I *received* from the Lord what I also *passed on* to you..." (1 Corinthians 11.23) .

- "For what I *received* I *passed on* to you as of first importance: that Christ died for our sins, according to the Scriptures..." (1 Corinthians 15.3).

- "Whatever you have learned or *received* from me, or seen in me - put it into practice..." (Philippians 4.9).

- "And we also thank God continually because, when you *received* the word of God, which you heard from us, you accepted it not as the word of men, but as it actually is, the word of God, which is at work in you who believe" (1 Thessalonians 2.13).

- "What you have heard from me, keep as the pattern of sound teaching, with faith and love in Christ Jesus. Guard the good deposit that was entrusted to you - guard it with the help of the Holy Spirit who lives in us" (2 Timothy 1.13).

•"And the things you have heard me say in the presence of many witnesses entrust to reliable men who will also be qualified to teach others" (2 Timothy 2.2).

If apostolic means coming from the Apostles, the question remains "What does it mean for us to be apostolic today?" I would suggest apostolicity may be found in three areas.

Apostolic Doctrine: We must hold to the same teachings the Apostles held to and transmitted to others. This is found primarily in the New Testament, but also in the early witness of the Church Fathers. If I want to understand more fully what the Apostles were saying, doesn't it make sense that I would turn to the men who were trained and ordained by them, most of whom, like the Apostles, gave their lives for sake of Jesus Christ?

Apostolic Practice: We must be committed to acting the way the Apostles acted. This includes ethics and morals based upon the Word of God, and it also includes a development of spiritual life in prayer, an openness to the power and presence of the Holy Spirit, and a commitment to share the

Gospel with others including those who are near us and those who are far off.

Apostolic Succession: A church that is catholic in the full sense should also be apostolic in its line of authority. That is, there should be an unbroken transmission of authority from the Apostles to the present leaders. Just as Paul ordained Timothy and Timothy ordained other leaders, the continuity of ministry has continued to the present day (this subject will be more fully addressed in the fourth book of this series, where we address the topic of ordination).

No single church group can lay claim to possessing the totality of all three of these apostolic qualities. With so many different groups and denominations - so many streams - it would be true to say that the Church is faithful to these qualities in degrees, but our goal should be to work toward that fullness "*until* we all reach unity in the faith and in the knowledge of the Son of God and become mature, attaining to the whole measure of the fullness of Christ" (Ephesians 4.12-13).

The Communion of Saints

The ancient and venerable doctrine of the communion of saints means two things.

First, it means that the saints (that is you and me and and everyone else who is in Christ) *share* (Latin *communio*, Greek *koinonia*) our lives with one another. We share our burdens and our joys, our laughter and our tears, our triumphs and our tragedies. We share our time, and our possessions. We also share those wonderful and sacred mysteries of our faith - the Word and Sacraments and presence of the Holy Spirit. One of Saint Paul's favorite phrases was "one another":

- "Be devoted to one another" (Romans 12.10).
- "Honor one another" (Romans 12.10)
- "Live in harmony with one another" (Romans 12.16).
- "Love one another" (Romans 13.8).
- "Stop passing judgment on one another" (Romans 14.13).
- "Accept one another" (Romans 15.7).
- "Instruct one another" (Romans 15.14).
- "Greet one another with a holy kiss" (Romans 16.16).

And these just from one of Paul's letters! He uses the phrase in regard to Christian relationships a total of eighteen times! A thorough study of the "one another" passages of the New Testament would provide a good understanding of the first meaning of communion of the saints - that we share our lives together because all our lives are in Christ.

But there is another idea contained in the communion of saints. Not only do we share our lives with one another - those of us who happen to be living on the earth at the same time - we also share our lives with *all* who are in Christ! My life is shared with Saint Paul himself. And with good old Saint Ignatius. And Saint Patrick. And the Blessed Virgin Mary. And my grandparents who are dead in this world but alive in Christ. The point is this: there aren't *two* Churches, one on earth and one in heaven. There is *one* Church - and its location is "in Christ." Let me give you one small example. My maternal grandmother was a godly woman who died in 1983. She is the one who gave me a love for reading and learning. I loved her dearly and miss her much. But I am still *connected* to her in some mysterious way. For you see, when she died, her spirit ascended to the heavenly realm and she became "present with Christ" (Philippians 1.21-22). But that is also where I am: "And God raised us up with Christ and seated us with him in the heavenly realms in Christ Jesus" (Ephesians 2.6)! Granny and I are both "in Christ". We do now and will forever share a union with one another because we share a union with Jesus Christ in the heavenly realms.

The Church on earth (called "the Church Militant") is not in the battle alone. We are joined by those who have by earthly standards died - but who are truly alive before the throne of God (called "the Church Victorious). And they are praying for us and rooting for us and cheering us on: "Therefore, since we are surrounded by such a great cloud of witnesses, let us throw off everything that hinders and the sin that so easily entangles, and let us run with perseverance the race marked out for us" (Hebrews 12.1). People often lightly say, "Heaven help us!", never realizing that heaven does help us - the saints around the throne, the angels, and all the heavenly host are joined in union with God himself - Father, Son and Holy Spirit - to help us walk in victory until that great day when all is made new.

Chapter Eleven

The Forgiveness of Sins

Apostles' Creed:
"The forgiveness of sins."

Nicene Creed:
"One baptism for the remission of sins."

"The forgiveness of sins". The phrase is
not used one single time in the Old Testament.
In the New Testament it becomes the central
message. In Luke the resurrected Christ
opened the minds of the disciples to what was
written of him and then the last thing Jesus
said to them was, "This is what is written: The
Christ will suffer and rise from the dead on the
third day, and repentance and *forgiveness of sins*
will be preached in his name to all nations,
beginning at Jerusalem. You are witnesses of
these things. I am going to send you what my

Father has promised; but stay in the city until you have been clothed with power from on high" (Luke 24.46-49). These are the marching orders of the Church. This is the message of Christ, the message of the Apostles and our message - that in Christ is found the forgiveness of sins.

Why So Serious?

In the Old Testament people offered blood sacrifices for their sins, but it never did work. Think about it - you commit some great sin against God, feel bad about it, intend to change your ways, so you kill an animal and give God the blood - that pays for everything? No way! In fact, the New Testament tells us that all those sacrifices were *reminders* of our sinfulness. All the blood sacrifices in the Old Testament were pointers - signposts - showing (a) that humanity was in a mess and (b) that *something* had to happen to deal with the mess. God directed the people of Israel to offer the blood of bulls and goats as a symbol of what that something was - the only sacrifice in the whole world that was really a sacrifice sufficient enough to *once and for all* deal with sin - the sacrifice of *himself* for us : "But those sacrifices are an annual reminder of sins, because it is impossible for the blood of bulls and goats to take away sins. Therefore, when Christ came into the world, he said: 'Sacrifice and offering you did not desire, but a body you prepared for me; with burnt offerings and sin offerings you were not pleased. Then I said, "Here I am - it is written about me in the scroll - I have come to do your will, O God."' First he said, 'Sacrifices and offerings, burnt offerings and sin offerings you did not desire, nor were you pleased with them' (although the law required them to be made). Then he said, 'Here I am, I have come to do your will.' He sets aside the first to establish the second. And by that will, we have been made holy through the *sacrifice of the body of Jesus Christ once for all*"(Hebrews 10.3-10).

Humanity - since the story of Adam and Eve in Genesis 3 - has been estranged from God. Not by God's doing, mind you, but by mankind's insistence on valuing it's own self-centeredness and independence over a true relationship with God. From the beginning God has sought to restore that relationship. But, like any real relationship, offenses had to be "dealt with". The only problem was, humanity was incapable of dealing with it. The whole race of man had fallen off the wagon and couldn't get back on by itself. It had no ground to stand on. It was in bondage to sin and to death and couldn't free itself or remedy the problem. *So God became one of us.* OK. Here is where you stop and ring the bells and shout a loud *Alleluia!* and get up and do a little dance! GOD BECAME ONE OF US! The One from whom we were estranged (by our own doing) became one of us in order, as a perfect man, to die an imperfect man's death: "God made him who had no sin to be sin for us, so that in him we might become the righteousness of God" (2 Corinthians 5.21).

The Big Picture

What God accomplished in Jesus Christ was not just the forgiveness of individual sinners - you, me, him, her, and them over there. He accomplished a fundamental realignment of the whole of humanity (and for that matter creation) in relationship to himself. When Saint Paul summarized the Gospel message in a sentence he said it best: "that God was *reconciling the world* to himself in Christ, *not counting men's sins against them*" (2 Corinthians 5.19).

What happened on the cross was bigger than the incidental and continual forgiveness of the individual sins of individual sinners. He took away the sins of the world! What the prophets had looked forward to, what John the Baptist had proclaimed, and what Jesus

164

accomplished was the changing of an entire paradigm. A new way of doing business, or better yet, a way of just closing shop on the whole business of sin itself.

Too many Christians (and too many "in it for the religion" churches) mistakenly think they relate to God through some transactional process of spiritual manipulation. If I say the right prayers, if I go to confession, if I kneel by my bedside and confess my sins every night before sleep, if I do A, B, C and D, then my doing these things will cause the great machinery of forgiveness to go into motion and the end result is that I will get my gum ball of forgiveness that lasts for the moment, and tomorrow I will do the same thing all over again. But what Christ accomplished for us was the "taking away" of the sins of the world. His sacrifice, once offered, was a full, perfect, sufficient and effective sacrifice for all sins. Period. The deal is done. There are no more transactions because the *great transaction* has already occurred! But wait! There is more!

The forgiveness of sins was what John the Baptist pointed to (Mark 1.4), Jesus shed his blood to secure (Matthew 26.28), and the Apostles proclaimed (Acts 2.38, 5.31, 10.43, 13.38, 26.18). In all these places the word for forgiveness is *aphesis*, and it means the dismissal of a charge, the setting free of the accused, and the the exclusion of punishment!

Now, to the really good stuff. As if everything we've seen so far wasn't enough, there is a very important point to notice in all the texts where the phrase "forgiveness of sins" is used (and while it isn't used once in the Old Testament it is used twelve times in the New): in all cases, the word forgiveness is in the *singular*. One. Once. A single forgiveness of sins. Stop reading for a minute and *think* about this.

OK. Done? Did you get it? There is one single *aphesis* of sins; one single forgiveness; one single dismissal of charges, freeing of the accused and removing of punishment. The thing isn't transactional. It has already been done! When Jesus died on the cross he really did take away the sins of the world. A lot of church folk are scared silly of this notion because they are in the business of (and make their money by) making people afraid of God and in one way or another selling them perpetual doses of forgiveness (the sales of indulgences in the Middle Ages serve as a good example, but it still happens in more subtle ways today - and across the board denominationally). But in Christ the reconciliation of the world and the taking away of sins has already occurred. Hebrews says it best: "But now he has appeared once for all at the end of the ages to *do away with sin* by the sacrifice of himself" (Hebrews 9.26). Christ has "done away with sin"! So what is left?

Be Reconciled

If Christ has already taken away the sins of the world (and he has), and if he has already reconciled the whole world to himself (and he has), then why bother with Christianity at all? There are several answers to the question and we don't have time or space to deal with them all, but an important one is this: God has created us as free agents. He has given us free wills. He created us to love him, and something can't love if it is forced to. Love must have the option of not loving. So, although he has completely dealt with our sins and has reconciled the world to himself, he isn't shoving it down anyone's throat. Instead he is inviting anyone and everyone to say "Yes" to what he has done. Right after Paul defines the Gospel as God in Christ "reconciling the world to himself, not counting men's sins against them", he says two more things. First, that he is called to be an ambassador, an announcer, of this good news, and secondly, that his plea is, "We implore you on Christ's behalf: *Be reconciled* to God" (2 Corinthians 5.20). Reconciliation takes two. God has done his part. He is not waiting for people to come begging forgiveness, he is running toward them with an overabundance of forgiveness spilling out of his arms wanting them to say "Yes" to his gracious love, and he has conscripted the whole lot of us believers to help spread the word. It's not for nothing that it's called the Gospel, "The Good News"!

But What About...?

I knew you would ask that. But what about all the passages in the Bible that tell us - Christians - believers - already-saved-folk - that tell us to confess our sins and repent of our sins? What about the passages that tell us that if we say we have no sin we are liars and the truth is not in us?

First, about the word confess. Our guilt-ridden-religion-is-about-transactionalism minds hear the word "confess" and automatically think it means "fessing up to misdeeds". In the vast majority of occurrences in the New Testament, it means no such thing:

> •"That if you *confess with your mouth, 'Jesus is Lord,'* and believe in your heart that God raised him from the dead, you will be saved" (Romans 10.9).

•"Men will praise God for the obedience that accompanies your *confession of the gospel* of Christ" (2 Corinthians 9.13).

•"At the name of Jesus every knee should bow, in heaven and on earth and under the earth, and every tongue *confess that Jesus Christ is Lord*, to the glory of God the Father" (Philippians 2.10-11).

•"Fight the good fight of the faith. Take hold of the eternal life to which you were called when you made your *good confession* in the presence of many witnesses. In the sight of God, who gives life to everything, and of Christ Jesus, who while testifying before Pontius Pilate *made the good confession*, I charge you to keep this command without spot or blame until the appearing of our Lord Jesus Christ" (1 Timothy 5.11-14).

•"Everyone who *confesses the name of the Lord* must turn away from wickedness" (2 Timothy 2.19).

•"Fix your thoughts on Jesus, the apostle and high priest *whom we confess*" (Hebrews 3.1).

•"Through Jesus, therefore, let us continually offer to God a sacrifice of praise—the fruit of lips that *confess his name*" (Hebrews 13.15).

Our primary confession is the confession of Jesus Christ as Lord and Savior! Only secondarily, and in only two places, are we told to confess our sins: "Therefore *confess your sins* to each other and pray for each other so that you may be healed" (James 5.16), and "If we *confess our sins*, he is faithful and just and will forgive us our sins and purify us from all unrighteousness" (1 John 1.9).

To confess means "to say the same thing as" (*con* - with, and *fess* - say; "to say with"). What does God say about our sins? Two things: we have them, and he has dealt with them. When we confess our sins, we are saying with God that, yes, we have these sins, and they are bad, and we despise them, and we want to be free not only from their penalty but also from their power and presence, and that, furthermore, God has already dealt with them on the cross of Christ! He has taken away their penalty, he is in the process of taking away their power, and he will ultimately take away their presence.

Why should you confess your sins, either to God, or to someone else, or sacramentally to a priest? Because it is an action of applying what God has already accomplished. We don't confess our sins for God's sake, we confess our sins for our sake - to bathe in the once and for all sacrifice of Christ, to take another step of making freedom from sin not just a positional reality, but a practical reality in our lives. Confessing sins frees us from their power in our lives. But it must be clear that confessing our sins is not pulling a transactional lever in order to get something from God. He's already given us complete forgiveness. Which leads me to the final thing.

One Baptism for the Forgiveness of Sins

Whereas the Apostles' Creed simply says I believe "in the forgiveness of sins", the Nicene Creed expands it to, I believe in "one baptism for the forgiveness of sins". While this is not the place for a thorough study of baptism, a few things need to be said about this sacrament.

First, there is "one baptism". The one baptism is first and foremost the baptism of Jesus himself. When Jesus stepped into the waters of the Jordan River he began the great exchange which would reach its culmination in his death, resurrection and ascension. He took our place. John was baptizing "for the forgiveness of sins" and Jesus had no sins to be forgiven. At first John refused to baptize him until Jesus said, "Let it be done...to fulfill all righteousness" (Matthew 3.15). How was all righteousness fulfilled? By Christ exchanging his own righteousness for our sins. We've already seen what Saint Paul said: "God made him who had no sin to be sin for us, so that in him we might become the righteousness of God" (2 Corinthians 5.21). Remember, then, that John the Baptist's proclamation related to Jesus' baptism was, "Behold, the Lamb of God, who *takes away the sin of the world*" (John 1.29).

When Jesus went into the water, the water didn't purify him, he purified the water. He created a new sacrament that had effect, for it was (and is) infused with the presence of the Holy Spirit. *All our baptisms are contained in his baptism!* We are all "baptized into Christ and have put on Christ" (Galatians 3.27). When we are baptized into Christ we are baptized into the realm of God's Kingdom of reconciliation, forgiveness and power. The sacramental door through which we enter the Kingdom of God is Holy Baptism. On the Day of Pentecost, when the people cried out to Peter asking what they must do to be reconciled to God, he replied, "Repent and be

172

baptized, every one of you, in the name of Jesus Christ for the forgiveness of your sins. And you will receive the gift of the Holy Spirit. The promise is for you and your children and for all who are far off—for all whom the Lord our God will call" (Acts 2.38-30).

We will study the sacrament of baptism in more detail in Volume Four of this series, but the thing to lay hold of now is that, contrary to much popular teaching, baptism was seen in the New Testament as the covenantal entry into the Kingdom of God. So much so that in all instances, salvation, the forgiveness of sins, the reception of the Spirit, membership in the family of God, and the sacrament of baptism are a unified whole, it being unimaginable to the Apostles that one of these should stand alone from the others.

The forgiveness of sins is not transactional. Baptism is not magical. Both are rooted in the person and work of Jesus Christ. In him, and him alone, is reconciliation with God achieved.

Chapter Twelve

The Resurrection of the Dead

Apostles' Creed:
"The resurrection of the body, and the life everlasting. Amen."

Nicene Creed:
"And I look for the resurrection of the dead: And the life of the world to come. Amen."

We come now to the end of the Creeds. Everything thus far has dealt with the past and the present. The final lines point to the future, and so the Creeds both end on a note of hope - a hope that is rooted in what God began in creation, what he redeemed and reconciled on the cross, and what he began bringing into fruition in the resurrection of Jesus. Note that what the Apostles' Creed makes the subject of belief, the Nicene Creed makes a matter not only of belief, but of anticipation: "I *look for* the resurrection of the dead..."

The Resurrection of the Body

The hope of the resurrection of the body is not a new thing with Christianity, but is found throughout the Bible. Job said, "I know that my Redeemer lives, and that in the end he will stand upon the earth. And after my skin has been destroyed, yet in my flesh I will see God; I myself will see him with my own eyes—I, and not another. How my heart yearns within me!" (Job 19.25-27), and Daniel wrote, "Multitudes who sleep in the dust of the earth will awake: some to everlasting life, others to shame and everlasting contempt" (Daniel 12.2).

Unlike the Greeks (and later heresies influenced by Greek philosophy), who taught that salvation was achieved by *escaping* the physical, the Bible and the Church believe salvation *includes* the physical. The redemption of the body is important because it shows the extent of God's reconciling work. He didn't come to save our souls. He came to save us totally - body, soul and spirit. He came to save creation itself.

The physical body is part of God's creation. G.K. Chesterton said, "The work of heaven alone was material; the making of a material world. The work of hell is entirely spiritual." When Christians start focusing on the spiritual to the exclusion of the physical, they step dangerously close to the early Gnostic heresies which ended up denying that God actually became flesh. God not only created all matter, he specifically and specially created the human body: "The Lord God formed the man from the dust of the ground and breathed into his nostrils the breath of life, and the man became a living being" (Genesis 2.7).

In the incarnation, God joined himself *forever* to matter, and specifically to the human body: "In the beginning was the Word, and the Word was with God, and the Word was God...the Word became flesh and made his dwelling among us..." (John 1.1,14). Notice, he did not simply assume flesh, he *became* flesh. In the resurrection Jesus was raised in a body: "Look at my hands and my feet. It is I myself! Touch me and see; a ghost does not have flesh and bones, as you see I have" (Luke 24.39).

The resurrection of our bodies is central to our redemption. The whole of Romans 8 and 1 Corinthians 15 bear reading in this

context, but notice particularly that Jesus'
physical resurrection, our physical
resurrection and the renewal of all physical
creation are intimately related: "And if the
Spirit of him who raised Jesus from the dead
is living in you, he who raised Christ from the
dead will also give life to your mortal bodies
through his Spirit, who lives in you" (Romans
8.11). "We know that the whole creation has
been groaning as in the pains of childbirth
right up to the present time. Not only so, but
we ourselves, who have the firstfruits of the
Spirit, groan inwardly as we wait eagerly for
our adoption as sons, the redemption of our
bodies. For in this hope we were saved"
(Romans 8.22-24; cf. also 1 Thessalonians
4.14, 1 Corinthians 6.14, 2 Corinthians 4.14,
Philippians 3.10-12).

When Will These Things Be?

The resurrection of our bodies, as we
have seen in Romans 8, awaits *the last day*,
when creation itself shall be renewed along
with us; that is, *all* the physical creation will
join us in our own resurrection! Here is not
the place for a detailed study of eschatology,
but the promise of the Bible - from Job to
Daniel to the New Testament - is that our
resurrection happens at the end of history (not

a thousand years before) and at the beginning of the remade heavens and earth. When Jesus came late to the side of his friend Lazarus, and Mary and Martha informed him that he was already dead, "Jesus said to her, 'Your brother will rise again.' Martha answered, 'I know he will rise again in *the resurrection at the last day.*' Jesus said to her, 'I am the resurrection and the life. He who believes in me will live, even though he dies; and whoever lives and believes in me will never die. Do you believe this?' 'Yes, Lord,' she told him, 'I believe that you are the Christ, the Son of God, who was to come into the world'" (John 11.23-27).

Jesus specifically and repeatedly tells us when this will occur: "And this is the will of him who sent me, that I shall lose none of all that he has given me, but *raise them up at the last day.* For my Father's will is that everyone who looks to the Son and believes in him shall have eternal life, and I will *raise him up at the last day*...No one can come to me unless the Father who sent me draws him, and I will *raise him up at the last day*...Whoever eats my flesh and drinks my blood has eternal life, and I will *raise him up at the last day* (John 6.39-40, 44, 54).

Who Comes Out Of The Graves?

This promised resurrection belongs not only to believers, but to all. Those who believe (that is, those who believe the Good News that God was in Christ reconciling the world to himself; those who say "Yes" to his offer of mercy and forgiveness) will rise to glory, and those who reject Christ will rise to judgment. Jesus said, "A time is coming when *all who are in their graves* will hear his voice and come out —those who have done good will rise to live, and those who have done evil will rise to be condemned" (John 5.28-29).

The difference between the two groups (those who believe in the grace of God through Christ and those who reject it) is this: those who believe have already begun experiencing everlasting life - they have already tasted the life of the world to come, and their bodily resurrection is simply the continuation of their salvation process. Those who have rejected Christ experience the same resurrection, but it is the continuation of their condemnation - remember, Christ does not condemn them, but their rejection of his very offer of grace condemns them.

The Life Everlasting

When the Creeds speak of the life everlasting, they are speaking not of duration (although that is included), but of quality. The life everlasting is a new kind of life - one that begins when a person turns to Christ in faith. In John 5 Jesus told his listeners that a time was coming (in the future) when all who were in the graves would hear his voice and come out. But there is another time, which Jesus said had already come: "I tell you the truth, whoever hears my word and believes him who sent me *has eternal life* and will not be condemned; he *has crossed over from death to life*. I tell you the truth, a time is coming and *has now come* when the dead will hear the voice of the Son of God and those who hear will live" (John 5.24-25).

Jesus speaks here of two resurrections. The first resurrection is spiritual and the second is physical. Later, John will write, "Blessed and holy are those who have part in the *first resurrection*. The second death has no power over them..." (Revelation 20.6). The "second death" is the death of condemnation on judgment day. It has no power over those who put their trust in Christ, because whoever believes in him "will not be condemned" (John

5. 24), for "there is now no condemnation for those who are in Christ Jesus" (Romans 8.1).

Saint Paul makes it clear that everlasting life has already begun for those who put their trust in Christ:

> •"And God *raised us up* with Christ and seated us with him in the heavenly realms in Christ Jesus" (Ephesians 2.6).
> •"having been buried with him in baptism and *raised with him* through your faith in the power of God, who raised him from the dead" (Colossians 2.12).
> •"Or don't you know that all of us who were baptized into Christ Jesus were baptized into his death? We were therefore buried with him through baptism into death in order that, *just as Christ was raised from the dead* through the glory of the Father, *we too may live a new life*" (Romans 6.3-4).
> •"Since, then, *you have been raised with Christ*, set your hearts on things above, where Christ is seated at the right hand of God" (Colossians 3.1).

Those who put their trust in Christ's unfailing grace have already been spiritually resurrected and have already begun enjoying eternal life. Our physical resurrection is simply an ongoing work of our total transformation in him.

The Christian View of Death

The last lines of the Creeds portray a Christian view of death which is different from the world's. For many (especially atheists and secularists in our own culture) death is simply the end. Nothing remains after dying. There is no hope of a future life. The best we can hope for is that someone will remember us in this world. But Christians, while recognizing the reality of death, also recognize that for us it is but a kind of sleep, from which we shall awaken to a new glory.

You may remember Saint Ignatius from earlier in this book. He was trained and ordained by the Apostles, was the bishop of Antioch, and was arrested and taken to Rome for martyrdom. Before his death, he wrote this to the Roman Christians, "Not the wide bounds of earth nor the kingdoms of this world will avail me anything. I would rather die and get to Jesus Christ, than reign over the ends of the earth. That is whom I am looking for - the One who died for us. That is whom I want - the One who rose for us. I am going through the pangs of being born...Let me get into the clear light and manhood will be mine" (Romans 6.1,2). Now, *that* is a good Christian attitude toward death - Ignatius saw the pains of martyrdom and death as "birth pangs" - leading to him being born, ultimately, in the resurrection!

Of course, Saint Paul said much the same fifty years before: "For to me, to live is Christ and to die is gain. If I am to go on living in the body, this will mean fruitful labor for me. Yet what shall I choose? I do not know! I am torn between the two: I desire to depart and be with Christ, which is better by far" (Philippians 1.21-23). Death, though it is an enemy, is an enemy that has been (in Christ) and will be (in us) conquered and brought to nothing: "But Christ has indeed been raised from the dead, the firstfruits of those who have fallen asleep. For since death came through a man, the resurrection of the dead comes also through a man. For as in Adam all die, so in Christ all will be made alive. But each in his own turn: Christ, the firstfruits; then, when he comes, those who belong to him. Then the end will come, when he hands over the kingdom to God the Father after he has destroyed all dominion, authority and power. For he must reign until he has put all his enemies under his feet. The last enemy to be destroyed is death" (1 Corinthians 15.20-26).

The Nicene Creed says, "I look for the resurrection of the dead and the life of the world to come." Christians do not look toward that day with dread and fear, but with expectancy. We *look forward* to the life of the world to come because it is the "blessed hope" with which we are called (Titus 2.13). It is the exclamation point at the end of a glorious sentence: "We win. Here, and in the hereafter! AMEN!"

And so end the Creeds, each with a hearty "Amen!", "So be it!", "Make it so!", "This I believe." The word amen is from the Hebrew root word for *believe* and *trustworthy*. And so, the Creeds end the way they began: "I believe...Amen!"

Appendix One

The Athanasian Creed

The Athanasian Creed is a much more intricate and detailed document, which is traditionally read in churches on Trinity Sunday, the Sunday after Pentecost Sunday. It is best read slowly and thoughtfully.

Whosoever will be saved,
before all things it is necessary that he hold the Catholic Faith.
Which Faith except everyone do keep whole and undefiled,
without doubt he shall perish everlastingly.

And the Catholic Faith is this:

That we worship one God in Trinity, and Trinity in Unity,

   neither confounding the Persons,

   nor dividing the Substance. For there is one Person of the Father,

   another of the Son, and another of the Holy Ghost.

   But the Godhead of the Father, of the Son, and of the

   Holy Ghost, is all one, the Glory equal, the Majesty co-eternal.

   Such as the Father is, such is the Son, and such is the Holy Ghost.

   The Father uncreate, the Son uncreate, and the Holy Ghost uncreate.

   The Father incomprehensible, the Son incomprehensible,

   and the Holy Ghost incomprehensible.

   The Father eternal, the Son eternal, and the Holy Ghost eternal.

   And yet they are not three eternals, but one eternal.

   As also there are not three incomprehensibles, nor three uncreated,

   but one uncreated, and one incomprehensible.

So likewise the Father is Almighty, the Son Almighty,
and the Holy Ghost Almighty. And yet they are not three
Almighties, but one Almighty.

So the Father is God, the Son is God, and the Holy Ghost is God.
And yet they are not three Gods, but one God.
So likewise the Father is Lord, the Son Lord,
and the Holy Ghost Lord. And yet not three Lords, but one Lord.

For like as we are compelled by the Christian verity to acknowledge
every Person by himself to be both God and Lord,
So are we forbidden by the Catholic Religion to say,
There be three Gods, or three Lords.
The Father is made of none, neither created, nor begotten.
The Son is of the Father alone, not made, nor created, but begotten.
The Holy Ghost is of the Father and of the Son,
neither made, nor created, nor begotten, but proceeding.

So there is one Father, not three Fathers;
one Son, not three Sons;
   one Holy Ghost, not three Holy Ghosts.
   And in this Trinity none is afore, or after
other;
   none is greater, or less than another; But
the whole three Persons
   are co-eternal together and co-equal.
   So that in all things, as is aforesaid,
   the Unity in Trinity and the Trinity in
Unity is to be worshipped.
   He therefore that will be saved is must
think thus of the Trinity.

   Furthermore, it is necessary to
everlasting salvation that he also
   believe rightly the Incarnation of our
Lord Jesus Christ.
   For the right Faith is, that we believe and
confess,
   that our Lord Jesus Christ, the Son of
God, is God and Man;
   God, of the substance of the Father,
begotten before the worlds;
   and Man of the substance of his Mother,
born in the world;
   Perfect God and perfect Man,
   of a reasonable soul and human flesh
subsisting.

Equal to the Father, as touching his
Godhead; and inferior to the
Father, as touching his manhood; Who,
although he be God and Man,
yet he is not two, but one Christ;
One, not by conversion of the Godhead
into flesh but by taking of the Manhood
into God;
One altogether; not by confusion of
Substance,
but by unity of Person. For as the
reasonable soul
and flesh is one man, so God and Man is
one Christ;
Who suffered for our salvation,
descended into hell,
rose again the third day from the dead.
He ascended into heaven, he sitteth at the
right hand of the Father,
God Almighty, from whence he will come
to judge the quick and the dead.
At whose coming all men will rise again
with their bodies
and shall give account for their own
works.
And they that have done good shall go
into life
everlasting; and they that have done evil
into everlasting fire.

This is the Catholic Faith, which except a man believe faithfully,
he cannot be saved.

Appendix Two

Suggested Reading

The *Apostolic Fathers* is a collection of the writings, primarily epistles, of the first generation of Church leaders after the Apostles, including Polycarp of Smyrna, Ignatius of Antioch, & Clement of Rome. In various editions.

Robert Capon's three volumes on the Parables (*The Parables of the Kingdom, the Parables of Grace, & The Parables of Judgment*) serve as a stunning introduction to his insights to the grace of God which permeate the New Testament.

C.S. Lewis' *Mere Christianity*, though only a half century old, is a global classic on what Christians believe, written in Lewis' insightful and beautiful style. A masterpiece.

Thomas Oden's three volume systematic theology (*The Living Word, Life in the Son and Life in the Spirit*) is probably the single best systematic theology in print. Literally every page quotes the ancient fathers of the Church as well as offering the best in modern scholarship.

N.T. Wright's *Surprised by Hope* offers a refreshing and brilliant overview of what the Bible teaches about the resurrection of the dead on the last day, and what it does *not* say about "going to heaven". I cannot recommend this book enough. I wish every Christian would read it.

Robert Webber & Timothy Johnson teamed up to write *What Christians Believe*. Written as a small systematic theology, it addresses each topic by looking first at what the Scriptures say, then giving an overview of how the Church has variously understood the given subject throughout the centuries.

About the Author

Kenneth Myers was born in 1959 in Denison, Texas. The son of a pastor/missionary, he married Shirley McSorley in 1977. They have three children and two grandchildren. He is an Anglican bishop and pastors Christ Church Cathedral in Sherman, Texas.

www.kennethmyers.net